READING PUSHKIN *in* SIBERIA

And Other Tales of Survival

CELIA N. ORES

ISBN: 978-1-4834-4946-3 (sc)
ISBN: 978-1-4834-4947-0 (hc)
ISBN: 978-1-4834-4945-6 (e)

Lulu Publishing Services rev. date: 04/29/2016

To my family who are my joy in life --

Pauline, Michael, Lia, Marisa, David, Michelle,
Chip, Adam, Paul & Marc

Contents

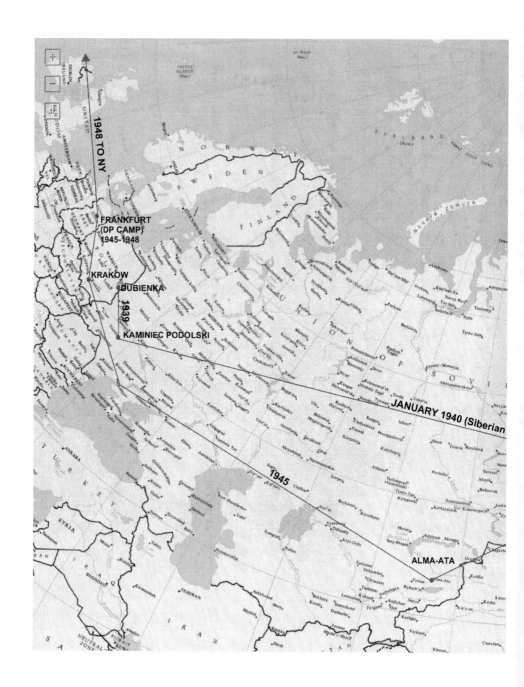

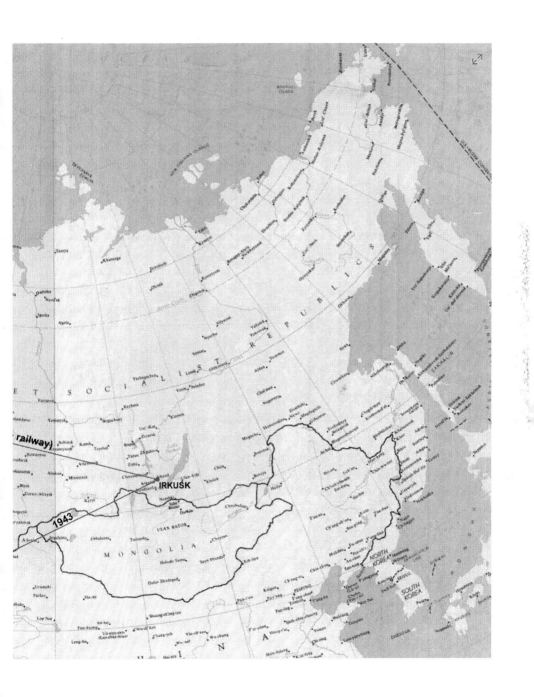

Foreword by My Grandchildren

By Adam Schorin

The first time I visited Dubienka, I was nine years old and my grandmother had both her original knees intact. We—Grandma, Mom, my cousin Lia, and I—walked around the town, visited the foundation of the synagogue (now next to a bus stop), spoke with a man who had lived through the war, and ate cherry blintzes (or something that resembled blintzes) at the home of a woman we referred to alternately as Barbara and Gabriela (one was her first name and the other was her middle name and nickname, but we couldn't remember which was which). At some point that day (we were only in Dubienka for a handful of hours), we walked to the banks of the River Bug, which Grandma had been ferried across at night sixty-five years before, fleeing German-occupied Poland to what is now Ukraine.

In my memory (which has been compromised by years of repeated visits), Grandma and I walk a few minutes down the riverbank and then she stops me. "Here," she says, "here is where we escaped."

Even then, in 2004, at age nine, I thought this was the most significant thing that had ever happened to me. When I returned to Dubienka this past summer, in 2015, without my family, I walked behind a group of high school kids carrying pool toys (an inflatable shark, a black and gray tube, a plastic mattress) to play with in the same river. One of them looked back and saw me on one knee focusing my camera, and they walked away.

I spent this past summer, through a grant from school, researching the Holocaust and retracing, in Poland, Germany, and Russia, parts of my grandparents' journeys through the war. I met with genealogists in Warsaw, sifted through photographs of my grandfather in Krakow, and had Shabbat dinner with the elderly members of the synagogue in Irkutsk, the Siberian city in which my grandmother was transported from train to truck, which carried her some hours north to the gulag. I went to a music festival in western Poland called Woodstock with a Hasidic Jew from Borough Park, and I spoke Hebrew with the granddaughters of a Ukrainian Jew on the Siberian island of Olkhon, in Lake Baikal. I had a beer in the synagogue in Chelm, now converted into the frontier-themed McKenzee Saloon, complete with Oregon Trail wagons and smiling cacti—and located down the street from where my great-grandfather was bar mitzvahed.

The Dubienka of today hardly resembles the one of my grandmother's stories. It has basketball courts and lottery machines, stop signs and traffic circles. The headstones that were stolen from the Jewish cemetery (and used as building materials, door stops, and, most viscerally, as cutting boards) have been returned, dumped haphazardly back into the cemetery, protected by a newly erected gate. My grandmother's childhood home is now a community center; her bedroom is part of its second-floor library.

I went back to the riverbank this trip as well, and was surprised to see how short a distance it was to the other side. In my memory, it had been like looking across an ocean, spying on New Jersey from the Upper West Side. Beer cans and cigarette butts littered our sandy, muddy bank, and when I walked back to the car, I slipped in a puddle and almost lost my sandal to the sludge.

For as long as I can remember, my grandmother has told me stories about her childhood, about fleeing Dubienka, about Siberia and Kazakhstan and her brother's death and the doctor who taught her Russian in the gulag and the officer who took her and her father to see the Soviet National Ballet perform Swan Lake in Alma-Ata in 1944. ("The prima ballerina was Galina Ulanova, and she was the most excellent dancer like nothing you have ever seen.") I've heard these stories thousands of times, always with the same pacing, the same inflection: "Mr. Kellner was, as my mother would have said, a mensch." In fourth grade I recorded her stories on a series of cassette tapes labeled "Dubienka 1-4," and I thought that would be it: I'd have her stories down and they would never be lost.

But it's not enough to hear them once. Each time I've turned to her stories, I've had more questions, more names and cities and people I want identified. And sometimes Grandma will tell a story I think have heard at least a hundred times before, and I'll be saying the last lines along with her, when all of a sudden she'll add something new, some detail she'd never included before or had just remembered herself. Like a novelist who sheds a little more light on her protagonist's secret past with each chapter, every now and then Grandma pulls back the curtain on her history a little bit further. Just this past summer I learned she spent a few days in a nunnery before her family decided to flee Dubienka.

"What? A nunnery?" I said. "You've never told me that before."

"I haven't? I only remembered it recently," she said. "The sisters taught me how to plant carrots."

Now we have the stories collected together, written and revised over the past 20 years. From familial memory to accessible history, the stories my siblings and I have told and been told our entire lives: all in one place, ready to be shared with anyone.

Heritage is a funny sort of thing. It can be evoked with the incantation of "pierogi" or "Lewandowski," or, perhaps, displayed in a museum. Often, it is kept dormant. Sometimes, it is the subject of a school assignment, the verification for an off-color joke, the way to enter a conversation you may not quite belong in. It can be stitched onto your sleeve. Yet, there is no measure of heritage more important than the stories of those who bear it. Celia Ores, my grandmother, does not have the same name she had at birth and lives thousands of miles from her shtetl of Dubienka in an apartment on the Upper West Side of Manhattan. Her Polish has been tinged with the accents of other relocated denizens, her neighbors and friends. She makes her kreplach with her strong and aged hands, and she tells the stories that time and place cannot extract from her. Sure, the details may be blurrier, the events that inspired them more distant, but the woman who tells them does her part in maintaining the most important teaching tradition in human history. And, unlike most lessons, the ones we can glean from my grandmother's stories do not have to be so clearly defined; it is up to us to value them as we see fit. Her stories are the heirlooms that matter, the ones that you can interpret for yourself, that change with each retelling. All we can do to learn from them is listen, and it is our imperative – as family members, friends, Jews, historians, anything – that we do. Those kreplach get looser each year. The rösti is no longer so easy to flip in the heavy pan. So read these stories with a compassionate eye, pass them on with careful tact, and let them linger in your head even as a culture of progress forgets them. That is what heritage is.

By Marc Schorin

Celia Ores, my grandmother, inspires. Her all-encompassing stories, her enveloping personality, her seamless resilience, every part of her teaches and gives. She has gifted so much to those around her, from passionate intellectual curiosity to a love and deep appreciation of literature and language. To be a part of her personal history — of a woman who survived the Holocaust and who, despite the many challenges of her being a woman, a Jew, and an immigrant, moved on to be a pediatrician and professor at a prestigious institution — is an overwhelming honor. I am excited to finally be able to share her life's story, with the hope that it will inspire others as it has me.

By Lia McCaffery

When I was 12, I visited my grandmother's hometown of Dubienka, Poland, with her, my aunt Michelle, and my cousin Adam, who was 10 at the time. I did not quite know what to expect, as I had heard some stories about her life before the war, but more about during her teenage years in Siberia and Kazakhstan, and her life as a pediatrician in New York. The village was surprisingly simple and quiet. Her home was in the center of the village but now used as a commercial space. We all walked to the River Bug, to where she crossed the river with her parents and brother Joseph to escape the Nazis' round up of the Jews the next day. For me, it was an easy stroll of a half-mile. But I could not imagine what the journey must have been like for my grandmother at age 12, in the middle of the night, being told to be absolutely quiet, without any belongings or knowledge of where or why you were going. It is just one small anecdote of how she survived the war. I am privileged to be her granddaughter and to be constantly inspired by her strength, kindness and courage.

By Marisa McCaffery

I have not personally known war or strife in my life. Even though our country has been at war for many years, I have been far removed from the conflict and fighting. In my grandmother's case, however, she was in Poland, directly in the middle of World War II. I had heard her horrific war stories, and then when I went to Poland last summer and I saw the Poland of today; it was difficult to juxtapose the Poland of wartime with today's Poland, making Celia's wartime experience all the more unfathomable. That she had emerged from that experience to become a caring doctor and loving grandmother is even more remarkable.

Introduction by Dr. John Schullinger

Here is the extraordinary memoir of a lady whose life story is one of indomitable courage and determination, of tragedy and triumph, of friendship and parental love, and love returned. You will read of her remarkable odyssey through the deprivations of her childhood and adolescence, through the unimaginable sufferings and hardships of war, persecution, and the Siberian wilderness, to her ultimate achievement as a devoted parent and physician. And not just any physician. Throughout her many years of practice and to this day I have never known another physician more selfless and caring nor one who was more loved and trusted by her patients and their families. She was there for them night and day, and in the end, when so many died the tragic death of the young, she continued to do whatever she could to alleviate their distress and comfort their parents. Her life was one of giving, and this memoir is, in a way, not only a gift to her family as a record of her life, but as a lesson for all of us to never give up, to do what is right, and to always be kind and generous to those who have little or nothing to give in return.

Anything more that I might say could only detract from Celia's own words. It has been an honor to have had for so many years the confidence and friendship of this truly distinguished and lovely lady.

This is her story. Hear what she has to say.

Chapter One

Dubienka: Before the War

I was born May 5, 1928 in Dubienka, Poland. I left when I was just 11 years old, but I remember the *shtetl* as a primitive yet vibrant place surrounded by forests and farms. There were several shops along the main street selling the shoes, fruits and vegetables, and baked goods that gave the town much of its character. Dubienka was located in the heart of Central Poland, but now it sits on the eastern border of the country, forty kilometers from Chelm and one hundred kilometers from Lublin.

In many ways, Dubienka was old-fashioned, even for the 1930s. There were only two cars in town—one for the mayor and one for another government official. When the mayor drove through town, children surrounded his car out of curiosity. Most people walked, or rode on horse and buggy along the cobblestone and dirt streets. The heart of our *shtetl* was a central square surrounded by shops and houses. There was a small park in the square across the street with a monument to General Kosciuszko where farmers sold their wares–produce, dairy and eggs at a weekly market. Wealthy landowners from Warsaw and Lublin leased their properties along the River Bug to the growers whose farms were equipped with horse-drawn ploughs.

We lived across the street from the town's central square on the second floor of a two-story brick building—the only brick building in town and the tallest in our village. I had a brother, Joseph, who was one of my closest childhood companions even though he was two years younger. We used to go to the park to throw balls around and go on the swing in the playground. Sometimes I jumped rope with friends from the synagogue. We began with a single rope and eventually learned to double jump with two ropes.

My father, Pincus Nuwendstern, was born in Chelm in 1903. He was a fine tailor and craftsman. He was meticulous, well organized and possessed impeccable taste. His *werkstadt*—tailor workshop—was located on the second floor of our apartment building, beside our living quarters. He employed about ten people who hand-tailored clothing. The Polish gentry from Warsaw, Lublin and Chelm who came to Dubienka every summer to check on the farmers tending their land were his best customers. They discovered that my father charged less than tailors in the cities, yet his work was just as good. The religious Jews of Dubienka, on the other hand, were of meager means. Most customers purchased just one *beckeshe*—a long black robe of three-quarters length—then wore it for life. Jewish fathers asked for Bar Mitzvah suits to be stitched with excess fabric for their thirteen-year-old sons so the sleeves and pants could be extended over time.

My father retained a tall and stately posture for all of his life, which he credited to his three years of service in the Polish army, from 1917-1920. He never had the opportunity for a formal education, but was always interested in world events, politics, and the goings on of the *shtetl*. He spoke Yiddish and Polish and kept up with local newspapers everyday.

At home we spoke both Yiddish and Polish, but mostly Yiddish. Because of his reputation for common sense and honesty, and his history of army service, Dubienka's town council selected my father as the only Jewish councilman. I would imagine that the townspeople didn't necessarily want to have "the Jew" on the council, but to my recollection municipal bylaws required a Jew.

In the wintertime, my father took Joseph and me to sled on the many snowy hills around town or to make snowmen with buttons for eyes in the park. He sometimes pulled our sled along the street. When we rolled the snow to form the base of snowman, he helped us push. It was a wonderful feeling to have his complete attention. He was a very busy man, so I relished the time he played with us. I felt protected with him.

I do not know much about my father's parents, Abraham Nuwendstern and Bluma Raizla (Szwarcberg) Nuwendstern, who were from Chelm, Poland. They died when he was a child, long before he moved to Dubienka. My father's two sisters were married and living elsewhere when I was young. His sister Anna Stelnick had been living in New York with her husband Benjamin and two children Abraham and Estelle. His sister Malka Rosenblum lived in Warsaw with her husband Leib and two children Cesia and Frank. After the war, Malka and her family built a new life in Montreal, Canada.

My mother, Ita Wajnstein, was born in Dubienka on May 12, 1905. Although her education was limited, she displayed tremendous *sechel*— common sense—as well as courage and conviction. She ran a furrier store on the first floor of our home, where she sold outerwear for men, including furs and jackets. Fridays, the day of the farmers market in the town square, were her busiest day. The farmers shopped at my mother's store because they appreciated her honesty and warmth. She was admired as one of the most beautiful and friendly women in town.

There was always work for my mother to do. In addition to running the store, she cleaned and cooked, kept a kosher home, shopped for groceries and cared for Joseph and me. In the winter, she piled wood

3

around the house, both outside on the balcony and inside in a special location in the hallway, to keep the stove running. During the summer and fall harvest, she canned vegetables and fruit, and made jams of all kinds, which she stored in an overflowing closet in the hallway. She ensured that we ate well through the bitter Polish winter.

We were by no means well off, but we were comfortable and well-cared for. In Dubienka, you could tell how wealthy families were by how often they did their laundry. The more often, the poorer. The wealthier townspeople only needed to wash laundry about once every two months because they had so many clothes. My mother washed our laundry roughly once a month. It was a complicated and dangerous process that she preferred we stay away from, but it piqued our curiosity. First, she filled a wooden *balia*—a tub—with water and bleach and soaked our clothes overnight. The next day she hired a local girl to help out. Together they boiled our clothing on the stove then scrubbed each article on a large washboard with soap and hung it all out to dry on the clothesline. My mother sent large items like sheets to the *mangle*—the machine in town that ironed laundry, and kept folds and creases from ruining precious fabrics. My mother ironed the rest by hand.

My mother's parents, Faygie and Abraham Wajnstein, lived in town, right on the River Bug, about half a kilometer from our home. Grandma Faygie baked challah every Friday in her large oven. She also fermented sour pickles, as well as sauerkraut. On Fridays, I walked to her home to pick up challah and glass jars of pickles for dinner. My grandmother also made little *pletzlach*—Polish flatbread sprinkled with dried onions and poppy seeds—that she baked on the sides of her oven. I recall she made us wait for the *pletzlach* to cool before eating.

My mother had three brothers – Shepsel, Fivel and the third name I cannot recall – who were all married and living in other cities in Poland. I had only met my uncle Shepsel Wajnstein from Bialystok, a town three hundred kilometers away (about four or five hours north by train). He manufactured glassware for pharmacies and must have been skilled at his craft, as he had a successful business. Shepsel and his wife Leah raised one daughter named Sonya, a very good pianist.

My parents considered sending me to live with my Uncle Shepsel's family to attend gymnasium—Polish secondary school. It was extremely difficult for a Jewish girl (or boy) to gain admittance to such schools, yet my uncle managed to enroll his daughter in Bialystok and offered to help my parents enroll me. He and my father thought this was my best chance to receive a good education. I had mixed feelings about potentially moving to Bialystok. I understood that I would have lived a more progressive life, but I would have been so far from my parents and my brother Joseph. I visited Bialystok a few times to get to know my relatives better. Their home was elegant and there was even a piano in the living room. However, the plans were never finalized as the war began before I was old enough to matriculate in gymnasium.

Jewish life in Dubienka was a central part of our lives. Out of a population of about 3,000 inhabitants, about 1,200 were Jewish, which included many children and quite a lot of the town's shop owners. That made the Jewish community roughly 40% of Dubienka's population. There were two synagogues and one church in town, as well as separate Jewish and Christian cemeteries. We were free to attend synagogue and Hebrew studies after school, but relations between Jews and Christians were not particularly friendly. The Church discouraged associations between the two groups, and we were not too eager to socialize with our gentile neighbors.

The Jewish community wasn't particularly diverse; there were very observant Jews and less observant Jews. My father was less observant, but he attended synagogue regularly to please his mother-in-law. Nor did he care if his kitchen was kosher, though my mother cared deeply and kept all the dietary rules.

The synagogue my family attended was beautiful and could seat several hundred congregants. It was not strictly Orthodox, but women sat upstairs, separate from the men. I remember there was a man who would sit outside the synagogue asking for *tzedakah*. I don't remember much about the rabbi except that he was an older man with a long beard who was well liked. I had heard that when congregants came to the rabbi's house to inquire whether or not a particular chicken was kosher, his Polish housekeeper, a gentile woman, opened the door and determined whether or not the bird was fit to eat or *treyf*.

Most weeks we hosted a guest or two for Shabbat dinner. There was a strong sense of camaraderie among the families of the synagogue. The rabbi often suggested that families of means should invite congregants who were alone or unable to cook for themselves to Shabbat meals. The kitchen smelled terrific on Friday afternoons. I didn't do much in terms of housework beyond thoroughly cleaning up on Friday and laying out a beautiful lace tablecloth. Sometimes we would go to Shabbat dinner at my Grandmother Faygie's; other times I would pick her and my grandfather up at their house a half-mile away and they would come to us for dinner. She would bring fresh challahs and rolls. We boiled water in a samovar on the balcony on Friday to have hot water until Shabbat ended on Saturday at sunset.

Shabbat was the time of the week when we ate richer foods that we didn't have during the week, like fish and chicken, matzo ball soup and usually cake. My mother made an excellent flourless poppy cake for Passover, which I still occasionally bake.

There was a very nice Jewish man who owned an ice cream and soda shop across the street from our home who gave out free ice cream so long as we helped him churn it. To promote Shabbat observance, he built a large brick oven in the back of his store for families to bring their *cholent*—Sabbath stew—which my mother made every week with beef, barley, beans and a hodgepodge of other ingredients. She prepared the stew at home in a ceramic pot, then covered the vessel with brown paper and wrote our family's name on it in pencil. I brought the pot to the communal oven behind the ice cream shop on Friday, but only an adult was allowed to retrieve the piping hot stew on Saturdays, after services.

We ate very well during the weekdays, too. On Fridays my mother went shopping at the farmers market for sour cream, butter, cheese, as well as the freshest fruit and vegetables. Each Friday she made cheese blintzes for lunch with the fresh cheese she bought. Blintzes were my favorite. When we came home from school we ate them with sour cream or homemade cherry, strawberry and gooseberry preserves. My mother also made borscht, red cabbage salad, kasha and potato latkes with sour cream or applesauce. In the mornings, she made chocolate milk and cooked farina or served fresh eggs with bagels from the bakery.

My father signed me up to attend Hebrew school in the afternoons. He chose Yavneh because it was a Zionist school that taught Hebrew, Bible, history of the Jewish people and Palestinography—the study of the geography of ancient Israel. All the kids were Jewish, but the school wasn't religious. I felt at home there. There was an Orthodox Yeshiva in town too, but girls weren't taught the same material as boys. My father thought Yavneh better suited me.

Public school was not nearly as comfortable for me. The majority of Jewish children did not attend the public school. There were very few Jewish children there with me to study Polish, the history of Russia, Germany and Poland, and mathematics from eight in the morning until two in the afternoon. I did have a friend in my class named Halina Golczewska. She was the daughter of a Polish Christian friend of my father's, whom he knew well from their service in the Polish army. At the time, her father operated a tobacco shop on the ground floor of my family's building. Halina and I jumped rope, sledded and studied together, but we were very different. She was blonde and Catholic, and I was neither. She performed the religious rituals during Catholic prayers in school while I sat alone to the side.

I always felt like the odd one out at public school, like an outsider. I faced discrimination regularly for being Jewish, from both students and teachers. Once, when I wore a white angora beret that my aunt Malka had given me, my teacher lifted it from my head and threw it into the fireplace in front of the whole class. Apparently it violated the dress code, which only permitted navy blue berets. I doubted that such a minor violation warranted that reaction. That same teacher stole a tablecloth I embroidered in school for my mother, who had asked me to stitch a red crisscross pattern on a large square of linen for her. It took me the whole semester. I was devastated because this was intended as a gift for my mother. I struggled to hold back my tears.

Anti-Semitism was in the air in Dubienka in the late 1930s, like a tense buzz of electricity, even beyond school. The priest in town promoted hatred against Jews from his pulpit. He was a horrible man. It was well known that he preached virulence against Jews, more aggressively about two years before Hitler invaded. He even forbade Catholic children from telling Jewish students what was taught during the Jewish holidays. When I asked my non-Jewish classmates for the work I missed while away, the children shook their heads and ran away. Even my friend Halina refused to help. The teachers made matters worse by always asking us about the material we missed during the holidays.

We never knew the answers and had to stand in the corner in front of the class, humiliated.

On Friday evenings, townspeople took their paychecks to the bar and drank heavily. This drinking often resulted in the harassment of the town's Jews. Most townspeople did nothing to stop this behavior, and sometimes encouraged it. Each year around Easter, the priest preached about the blood libel—the pernicious, anti-Semitic notion that the Jews kill Christian children for their blood to use in wine. We stayed away from the bars and stayed in on Friday nights and Easter. In synagogue, we heard about the various assaults that took place, which happened all too often.

The atmosphere in Dubienka became increasingly uncomfortable for Jews, although with the arrival of Hitler in 1939, these anti-Semitic events, although painful, paled in comparison to what was to follow.

Chapter Two

The War Begins

I was playing in the park near my house in September of 1939, when I heard the roar of planes overhead and the explosions of bombs dropping from the sky. I was eleven-years-old. A man—likely a German soldier—climbed a tree to attach a loudspeaker and then announced that war had begun. I ran home in fear.

I had been hearing whisperings of war from my parents and others, but no one had ever talked to me about it. War had seemed like a concept too distant, too foreign, and too *large* to arrive in our small town. But it did. And then we were instructed to head to our bomb shelter, but we had none. Fortunately the bombings were not extensive; my understanding was that they were merely intended to frighten the Polish people.

The German foot soldiers arrived a few days later, invading from the West while the Russians attacked Poland from the East. Within one week, Poland capitulated and was divided in two. The River Bug, which ran through our town, became the de facto border between German and Russian-occupied Poland. My family wound up on the German side by just one kilometer. Unfortunately, many of our Polish neighbors were all too pleased to welcome the Germans.

The sight of the German soldiers petrified us children far more than the falling bombs. The soldiers stood with perfect posture, wearing crisp uniforms, shiny boots, fitted hats and an obnoxious sense of superiority. They brandished sophisticated new weapons. The image of these perfectly attired soldiers frightens me to this day. People often wonder why Jews did not rebel until the Warsaw ghetto uprising. Those who ask have never seen those soldiers, nor witnessed how their commanders emphasized *ordnung über alles*—systems and order above all else.

The German soldiers were unbelievably cruel. I watched when a young girl, about four or five-years-old, failed to move out of a soldier's path. He picked her up and threw her against a tree, fatally wounding her. The image of the young girl still haunts me in the middle of the night. The soldiers' capacity for cruelty was unbelievable.

Each day over the course of a few weeks, the occupying Germans issued decrees, which included curfews and restrictions for the Jewish community of Dubienka. Officers paid Poles to translate the decrees and hang signs in the park and other public spaces. Day after day, more decrees were issued that had severe implications for the Jews of Dubienka.

Sensing the worst, my mother arranged for me to hide in a local convent for a few days. The nuns took a great risk upon their convent by admitting a Jewish girl at that time. I was lucky that I didn't look Jewish with my braids and light brown hair. There were two other Jewish girls and the nuns told us to separate from one another and not converse. The less you talk to each other the better, they told us. One girl came from surrounding farms and one was also from Dubienka. I learned how to cross myself and say prayers to fit in with the other Catholic 11-year-olds. I also helped with basic chores, like planting carrots in the garden. My mother took me from the convent after a few days to be together as a family as she sensed there was a possibility that we'd have to flee.

The Germans eventually decreed that all Jews were to report to the town center the following day. No other information was provided. My parents were incredibly anxious and had no sense of what would happen at the town center. My father felt we had no choice but to follow orders. If we didn't, he understood, we'd have to hide or run away. It was hard to hide in Dubienka since the Germans threatened to kill any Poles who hid Jews and offered rewards—either a bottle of vodka or a pound of sugar—to those who reported anyone concealing Jewish families. My father was also concerned about my mother's beloved three-door inlaid wooden wardrobe that she had specially made over the course of two years to store her linens and clothes. It was beautiful and expensive. "How could you leave the closet that you waited two years for?" he asked. "It's just a closet," she responded. She felt that no good would come from going to the square. She wanted to flee.

That night my mother connected with a Jewish man similarly wary of the most recent decree. He was a horse trader, a profession not regarded as *balabotish*—decent and trustworthy—in the Jewish community. He was referred to as a *gonif,* a thief. Yet he had an instinct for survival. He agreed to take us on his small boat to the Russian side of occupied Poland, across the River Bug. If the boat capsized, I am sure my father anxiously wondered, how was he going to rescue my mother, Joseph and me? He was the only good swimmer in our family. My mother was persistent, though, and we decided to flee as a family.

Off we went in the middle of the night. We walked to the river from our house. It was a long, frightening walk; we couldn't cough, sneeze, or make any sound. It was September so it was cool at night and an almost full moon reflected on the surface of the dark water. As we rode in the boat, I held on to my father for dear life, praying for the crossing to end.

If caught, we would have been shot instantly. It was risky for all of us, but especially for our rescuer, the horse trader. He endangered his life on our behalf. We later found out that after helping other Jews cross the river, he took his own family to the Russian side to escape. We were fortunate that my mother had a good sense about things to come and that we were able to successfully flee from the Germans.

My uncle in Bialystok was not as fortunate. We had heard that like us, he chose to flee, but his wife and daughter were attending the World's Fair in the United States when Germany invaded Poland. He wrote to them by post, begging them to stay put. They didn't heed his warning or didn't receive the message and returned home. With real urgency, he met them at Gdynia, the Polish port, and boarded another ship with them to the United Kingdom. When the UK did not permit their ship entry, their captain continued onward, toward the United States. While in transit, a German vessel torpedoed their ship.

We crossed the river to Russian-occupied Poland, and then made our way to the town of Kamenets-Podolsk, where my mother's other brothers lived, Fivel and the other brother whose name I cannot recall. We stayed in one of their homes. There were kids all over the place but I didn't want to play with them. I was shell-shocked from our escape and restless. I remember very little from this period of time. Food was scarce, though I had little appetite.

After a few months, in the winter of 1940, Russian soldiers appeared at the house with guns and bayonets in the middle of the night, and ordered us to leave the house within ten minutes. The soldiers told us to take whatever we were wearing and nothing more. My mother asked if she could dress her children, and they permitted it. While the Russian soldiers often demanded that we follow their cruel, unjust orders, they were overall more humane than the Germans.

The soldiers took only my family, leaving behind my uncles and their wives and children. They walked us to the train station where others who had crossed over to Russian-occupied Poland in search of sanctuary had been rounded up. We were all placed in a cattle car together with standing room only. Not once did the Russians tell us where we were going or why they chose us. This is how our struggle for survival over the next five years began.

Hitler later invaded Soviet-occupied Eastern Poland in the summer of 1941, about a year and a half after we were sent away. My uncles, their spouses and their many children who had housed and protected us were eventually massacred at Sobibor, a concentration camp near Lublin. In a bizarre twist of fate, Stalin and the Russian army that shipped us off to a great unknown—in the most inhumane conditions—wound up saving our lives.

Chapter Three

Survival in a Siberian Gulag

The Siberian railroad was a single-track line. We stopped at each station to allow trains coming from the opposite direction to pass. We could see that those train cars were hauling tanks and munitions, a sign that Russia was preparing for war.

There were about 150 people in each train car and eight or ten train cars altogether—about 1,500 people total. Our journey was long and arduous, roughly two weeks in all. We had no idea where we were headed, why we were chosen, or how long we would be in transit, which made it all the more difficult.

There was a soldier in each car handing out bread daily and granting us permission to drink *kipiatok* (hot water from a boiler) whenever the train stopped at a station. There was just a single spout from the *kipiatok* and only one pewter cup attached by chain. Over a thousand of us lined up at a time to drink.

As we passed the Ural Mountains, we came upon several overturned cars from another train—the remnants of an accident. Our convoy's soldiers permitted us to leave the train car to collect large tin cans (the size of paint cans) scattered along the tracks. A number of prisoners disembarked with nails and stones in hand to open them, discovering red caviar inside, which a few eagerly consumed. My mother warned

15

us to stay away. We had been malnourished since the start of the war, and the caviar would have been too rich for our empty stomachs, she told us. She gave us pieces of her bread ration instead. The eight or ten prisoners who ate a significant amount of caviar grew sick and died shortly thereafter. Soldiers buried their bodies beside the tracks. The trip continued.

During the trip I tried to make sense of the situation. I pestered my father with questions: "Are we bad people? Why were we treated like flies? Did we commit a crime?" *There must be a reason for all of this,* I thought.

He explained repeatedly that in countries around the world, the Jewish people have been persecuted and blamed for things they have never done. Anti-Semitism is not logical or humane, he reiterated. We are an easy target with no country of our own and no one to protect us.

After weeks of travel by train, we stopped at Irkutsk, the last station stop in what we soon learned was Siberia. We boarded a boat to cross the Lena River, then tightly packed onto the back of a flatbed military truck for a long trip, until finally we walked on foot for a good distance toward our final destination: a labor camp in the Gulag.

Gulag is technically an acronym for the Russian organization that ran the labor camps in Siberia, but for all intents and purposes, a gulag is a forced labor prison camp in the midst of the vast Russian wilderness, and many of these labor camps were east of Irkutsk. Guards were stationed all around and forced labor, combined with harsh weather, led to much death and despair. To survive time in a gulag is a highly emotional experience, one that changed my life forever.

Our labor camp was situated in an open area of the dense woods with only six big log cabins for the 1,500 prisoners who were forcefully relocated there. Trees surrounded us on all sides except at the entrance, where there was a fence – and guards who weren't terribly good at their jobs. Occasionally they would make a prisoner stand-in for them. It didn't matter. There was no chance of escape from the middle of nowhere. Where could we go? The winters were unbearably cold, so for three-quarters of the year it was too dangerous to venture into the wilderness. And the summer was too short to get very far. The entire gulag drew water from the same well. In each of the several cabins, we shared just one bucket of water. Children were official water collectors. When the water in the buckets froze during wintertime, we chipped through the layers of ice to access the water beneath.

To this day, I have such a clear picture of the log cabin without windows that became our new home. Sunlight peeked through the crevices between the logs. Our room held as many prisoners as could fit, about one hundred. We slept on raised wooden platforms covered with straw and riddled with lice. They permitted showers once a week, when they took our ragged clothes to sterilize them. It was difficult to understand why the attendant on the woman's side of the shower was always male, and female on the man's side. There was a rabbi with two daughters in our cabin room. One of the daughters named our gulag *Hotel Nenza*, meaning "the worst hotel."

Fortunately, each family was permitted to stay together. We felt very connected to the other prisoners and over time built a real community, a testament to the power of the human condition. And my father soon earned a great reputation. He was considered very reliable and trustworthy. When there was no one to hand out bread to the prisoners one day, he was selected.

17

Guards forced the adults to labor each day, whether they had the strength or not, usually cleaning the village grounds, or working with lumber, or digging graves in the forest. There was a special area for burials. Sometimes the guards created tasks to keep everyone busy, like cutting down trees, chopping wood to use at the Gulag, cutting wood to build structures, and sending logs down the river. The adults returned home from work tired and exhausted. The work was grueling, as were the conditions. Many of the prisoners died from exhaustion, hunger and the cold. I witnessed burials all the time in the forest. A rabbi among us officiated the burials until he passed away himself.

The whole situation made no sense. The work my parents were doing seemed completely arbitrary. We had heard that Stalin's excuse for putting many Jews in Siberia after crossing into the Russian side of Poland was that he believed Jews to be Hitler's spies. At some point the prisoners concluded that such a rationale was the only possible reason for sending us to Siberia. But there wasn't much discussion among the prisoners about our circumstances. What was the point? There were slight murmurs from time to time, but feelings of despair and disbelief had taken over.

A doctor named Galina Surshanskaya was assigned to the camp to watch over the prisoners. Her father was a Ukrainian landowner. Owning land was a crime in the Soviet Union, which is why she was sentenced to this remote prison with us. Our fates were intertwined with those of the guards. Galina became my saving grace. Not only was she young and beautiful, but she was exceptionally smart and very nice. She built relationships with many of the prisoners. My mother called her a *mensch*, a title she didn't bestow upon many people.

Our gulag's conditions presented Galina with a difficult task as a medical practitioner. There were so many illnesses and deaths, yet absolutely no medication to administer and no tools with which to treat any of us. The adults, as part of their forced labor, built an infirmary building with a white roof and a painted red cross, but the guards never stocked it with equipment. It was just for show. Galina had to rely on her wits. She became more of an advisor, teaching us how to prevent infections and to reduce frostbite during winter. She didn't know if water that was not boiled was safe to drink, so she taught us to only drink the *kipiatok* from the huge metal bowl (about 1.5 yards in diameter) atop a continuous fire at the center of camp, which kept the water boiling and scared bears away at night. She also taught us how to maintain healthy hygiene. When we scooped up water from the wooden pail in the well, we were instructed to walk the pail several yards to our cabin's bucket so filth would not contaminate our only water source.

Unfortunately, Galina had no control over the Russian guards, who increasingly became more abusive towards us as time went on. But she did try to make life at the Gulag more bearable for the children. When the adults worked during the day, she supplied us with twine to make jump ropes.

The guards, meanwhile, gave us nothing but bread to eat. It was hearty dark black bread, without anything to accompany it except *kipiatok*. One time the guards made us a cabbage soup. It was horrid, but we ate it. We stood in line daily to receive our ration of 500 grams, the size of a standard loaf of bread. The guards cruelly injected the bread with water so that they could give us less at the same weight. My mother offered me some of her bread ration each week. "Why are you giving this to me?" I asked her. "You need it, too." She replied, "You're growing and I'm not."

In the summer Galina tied us children together with a single rope around our waists and took us into the woods to forage for food. We couldn't go in more than a few feet because the forest was so dense, and we were told there were bears. We picked wild berries, raspberries and various mushrooms. We had to promise not to eat anything until she inspected our collection. We were warned that the most beautiful mushrooms, the *muchomor*, with red and white polka dots, were very poisonous. We washed the safe mushrooms then either ate them or cooked them over a fire in the one large metal bowl we all shared.

We were almost always swollen due to hunger and a lack of protein. One day my mother decided to leave the camp in search of food. She was warned, "If guards don't shoot you, the bears will get you." Determined to find nourishment for us, however, she departed early in the morning. When she returned later that day at dusk, she was carrying a bunch of beet greens, a sack of discarded potato peels (not actual potatoes) and a whole duck. She then set to work cleaning the whole bird using a borrowed knife from another prisoner. She added the duck, potato peels, beet greens and wild mushrooms to a pot of boiling water to make a soup.

My mother made sure everyone in camp had some before I could taste, but my turn did eventually come. It felt wonderful to have something warm to eat. It was only later that I noticed that my mother's rings—which she always wore on her fingers—were missing. She had bartered them to nourish us all. The rabbi refused to eat the soup, as the duck was not kosher; however, he told his daughters that he wouldn't sit in judgment if they chose to partake. They did. Soon afterward, he died of starvation, yet his daughters survived.

My brother Joseph had many friends with whom he played, even in freezing weather. I, on the other hand, chose to spend my free time learning with Galina. I was lonely. I spoke to some boys and some girls, but we didn't have much in common. Most children, including Joseph, weren't interested in learning. Children found other ways to pass time, like playing pebbles or jumping rope or playing with a ball that Galina fashioned. In the winter, the children made snowmen. When there were no games to play, they invented games for themselves.

Galina began teaching me the Russian language and writing from the books she was allowed to bring with her. I soon became skilled enough to read Pushkin, Lermontov, Gogol, Tolstoy, Turgenev, Dostoyevsky as well as translations of Shakespeare, Lord Byron and other masters. These works became my new outlets during the short, cold Siberian days, a way to temporarily escape the utter misery of my life. I could repress my feelings and frustrations into the books. I couldn't share my feelings with my parents because they felt awful, too. Galina gave me a long poem, "Eugene Onegin" by Alexander Pushkin, whose passages I read every evening and fully memorized by morning. I can recite it to this day. I grew so invested in Russian literature, and learned a lot about Russian culture from talking with Galina. But I had no one else to share my discoveries with besides her. Nobody cared, so I kept it all to myself. Galina became my only real friend.

It was difficult to read at night so Galina fashioned a lamp for me. She gave me a little glass bottle the size of a shot glass, put oil in it, then pulled a twig of cotton through the hole of a metal lid—and that was my lamp. She told me to read just one hour at night since she didn't have enough oil. She also warned me not to fall asleep while reading since the bed was made of straw and wood. I was grateful to have a lamp. At one point, I developed night blindness and Galina treated me by giving me carrots she miraculously found.

The forest was so thick that moisture accumulated so that mosquitoes thrived, which meant that malaria was a real threat. My mother eventually contracted the disease. She would shake every fourth day, a common symptom. Galina wrote a permission slip for her to get out of work so she could stay in the cabin during her malarial episodes. That was all she could do without medication to offer. My mother miraculously survived.

I felt very threatened by her illness, though. I loved her desperately. If anything were to have happened to her, I knew that our lives would have never been the same. She's the one who had the courage to go out and risk her life in order to find us nourishment. My father followed rules, but my mother did whatever she needed to do. She was the reason we had survived this long.

My brother was not so lucky. Galina diagnosed Joseph with meningitis. She was helpless without any medicine. We were all helpless. Two other young girls also contracted the illness at the same time. It was awful to watch. Joseph died at the age of ten and a half. We buried him along with too many others. One rabbi amongst us said a hastily spoken prayer. Not much else was said. My parents grew depressed and withdrawn. It was very hard for all of us.

Approximately two and a half years had passed when the guards announced we would be leaving the next day. It was the beginning of 1943. We didn't know exactly how long we spent in the Gulag because there were no calendars or papers or pencils with which to keep track of time. We were rounded up without word or reason yet again and placed in cattle cars. We were never told where we were going and we had no idea where we would be taken.

A young Jewish man, a fellow prisoner, was so in love with Galina that he asked her to come with us. "No," she said, "this is my country, for better or worse." I don't know what happened to her and I often still wonder. There's no way she could have stayed in touch with us, since Stalin did not approve of such communications.

I didn't want to leave Galina. She embraced me as I said farewell and we both cried. And then we left on the train. She gave me opportunities to learn and explore that I would never have had otherwise, and as a result, she became my closest friend. Without her I believe I would have been overwhelmed by my mother's illness, my brother's death and the harsh reality of the conditions of the Gulag. She was my salvation. People like her are very rare.

As we departed, we said farewell to my brother Joseph's modest grave that we had dug for him. Hundreds of others died in the Gulag, as well. Out of about 1,500 of us who arrived together, only 800 of us were aboard the train on our way to the next unknown prison, leaving the remnants of our fallen loved ones behind.

Chapter Four

The Deserts of Kazakhstan

After a few days by train, in cramped cattle cars, we landed in Sary-Ozek, Kazakhstan. I was about fifteen at the time. Again, we did not know the reasons for the transfer or the motivations of the Soviet Union. What we soon learned was that we were moved to a prison town very close to the Chinese border, about 150 kilometers from Alma-Ata (now Almaty), then the capital of Kazakhstan. As it turns out, we merely changed prisons and moved from Siberia's gulag to Kazakhstan's desert. There were Jews, Russians, Kazakhs and Mongols—all prisoners. I remember it was unbearably hot and there was nothing but sand and brush for days.

As far as prisons go, however, it was better than what we had in Siberia. Unlike the Gulag, where we lived in a cabin with a hundred other people, in Sary-Ozek we lived with just our family in a mud home. We even had our own stove in the house where we could boil water. Plus, the temperatures were no longer sub-zero.

But it was hard to adjust to the heat. It was nearly 100 degrees Fahrenheit every day. Sometimes it reached 105 degrees. The air was only tolerable in the early mornings, so we quickly learned to wake up early. That's when we went to collect the *sachsaul*, twigs with tiny little leaves from the desert necessary to feed cooking fires. I would collect

24

bundles of the twigs in my skirt. It was very dangerous to go out in the desert for too long without enough water. It was also tough for me to wake up that early, yet at four o'clock in the morning, it was peaceful and the desert steppes were quite beautiful. I liked that very much.

The Jewish people that came with us from Siberia were our constant companions. We shared many things; it was a village, after all. We were clustered together in hundreds of small houses. All of the prisoners in town lived in similar homes, with walls, floors, and ceilings made of mud. Each home had a bedroom, a side room with a stove and an outhouse.

We had only one snowfall the entire time we were there. I recall that one of our friends was worried the roof of her home might not support the weight of the snow, so she climbed atop to wipe it off. The roof collapsed and she fell into her house. She wasn't hurt, since the roof was only about a foot taller than my father, a moderately tall man.

We were given a ration of bread, a few apples from Alma-Ata and some grain. Water was hard to come by and was rationed at the well. My mother was a magician when it came to fixing up a good meal from ingredients that were so basic and meager. She only cooked for dinner. Sometimes it was grain and a piece of apple. But I was not as hungry as I was in Siberia. Perhaps it was the heat. Breakfast was a piece of bread. At times we had butter to spread onto it, which felt like a real luxury. And there was always a piece of apple to go with every meal.

There were different labor functions for the adults to do, but overall life was easier in Kazakhstan than in the Gulag. The work seemed less difficult.

Native Kazakhs also lived in this village. Well, the women lived in the village and the men led a nomadic life, returning quite often. Kazakh men were known as good horsemen. They wore leather pants with fur lining. They were poor people. They owned a few goats, seemed to only have a little more food than us and their mud homes were a bit larger than ours.

The Kazakhs saw me walk by everyday going to school. One day, a woman told me to come to dinner. She didn't ask, but she must have noticed that we had nothing significant to cook. Perhaps she felt sorry for me, or possessed what we would call *rachmunes*—pity. Such invitations were very uncommon since Kazakhs usually stayed to themselves. Only I was invited, though. I was afraid to go. My mother assured me that it would be all right and insisted that if I declined the invitation, they would be insulted. "You will eat what they give you and you'll thank them," my mother said, "and you'll have to eat the food whether you like it or not."

When I arrived at their home, I noticed the women sat quietly. I found it peculiar that in their home, the Kazakhs displayed a bed with beautifully embroidered pillows that nobody slept on. They all slept on the floor. But the quality of the embroidery was really impressive.

The women boiled water in a large cast-iron cauldron that had about a 3-foot diameter, similar to the cauldrons we used in Siberia but much smaller. Sitting on the floor cross-legged before a low table, they took dried goat meat hanging from a rope, swarming with flies, then cut it up into pieces, washed it off, and placed it in the cauldron to cook. Then the women took flour and water and made dough, which they rolled out on the table. They cut noodles and dropped them into the boiling water with the meat. Eventually they put out the fire, let it cool, and transformed the cauldron into the communal serving dish. Meanwhile, a woman handed me a metal mug of fresh goat milk. As soon as the noodle mixture had cooled, my hosts ate with their fingers. There were no utensils to be seen. I did what my mother told me to do and joined in, even though the whole experience was so foreign to me, and I didn't like the food or the way they were eating. Unfortunately, I became ill from the food, partly because I had not eaten meat for so long. To this day, I still hate goat cheese and avoid anything having to do with goats; I still associate the smell with that experience.

In retrospect, the Kazakhs were very kind. They admired my braids. They liked me. They didn't say very much, but the way they behaved showed real hospitality and kindness. Even though they were poor people, they gave me what they had, which was just a bit more than what I had. This was the only occasion I was invited. Afterward I'd say hello to them when I passed by from school, which made me feel better about living in the town. This was a highpoint of my time in Kazakhstan.

Perhaps the hardest adjustment for me to my new environment was the absence of Galina, my mentor and teacher. I missed her. Studying and learning with Galina was my saving grace during those hard times in Siberia. Fortunately for me, there was a very primitive school in our prisoner village with superb teachers.

As the Germans advanced and the front of the war moved closer to Moscow, the Soviet Union permitted older teachers ineligible for army service (and thus useless to the war effort) to leave Moscow for the hinterlands. Some of these teachers wound up in our village and taught mathematics, algebra, trigonometry, Russian literature and history at the school for prisoners. There was also an emphasis on Engels, Karl Marx, Lenin and Stalin, and other important Communist thinkers, as per Stalin's insistence. The government provided us with paper and pencils, tools we didn't have in Siberia. It was a new life for me at age sixteen.

Since I was fluent in Russian at this point and knew quite a bit about literature, thanks to Galina, I was better at school than other kids. When the teachers discovered I could speak and write in Russian, they were very pleased. I even told them I wanted to learn Ukrainian so I could read Taras Shevchenko, a poet I learned about from Galina. My father joked that I was a *yeshiva bocher*—a student of Talmud—and said that if I were given a bag of a thousand candy wrappers, I would read each and every one. I was insatiable. The more I learned, the more I wanted to know, like the periodic table and Lysenko's botany, which fascinated me. I came alive in school.

I knew many local kids from the school, but we weren't friends. It was tough to make friends in the Soviet Union since we were so guarded, unable to talk openly. My mother taught me to be careful when I speak, since nearly everyone could be listening on behalf of the Soviet government. My father told me that we could only talk openly about our work, so I limited my contact with the other students and just tried to be polite at school.

Most of the Jewish kids didn't attend school with me or even speak Russian. This distanced me from them. Not to mention that I had homework to do. I liked to take walks in the desert or jump rope with some local boys and girls. I also spent a lot of time with my parents, with whom I was very close. We ate all of our meals together and talked to one another. My father was prouder of my schoolwork than my mother, who thought a girl should get married and have children. My father was a strong proponent of my education, since he didn't have the opportunity for himself in Poland.

A few months after we were relocated to Sary-Ozek, the United States Army donated fabric for Russian officers' uniforms. The Russian Army divvied up the allotment to officers all over the Soviet Union. Officers in Sary-Ozek only received a small amount of fabric, so naturally they wanted to make as much use of it as possible, and held a contest to see which tailor could make a uniform using the least amount of fabric. My father entered the competition. A few days later he was notified that his design won. He was immediately taken off of hard labor and reassigned to tailoring, and given a special room to work in along with machines to operate. This was only a few months into living in our new home. Life was improving.

When the first uniform was finished, I thought the Russian officer who received it would faint. He had never worn a garment so well tailored and so comfortable. He came to our hut with a truck of *sachsaul*, the small twigs we collected to keep our fires ablaze, in addition to a pound of butter and some other goodies. My mother divided the gifts among our community, since we all looked out for each other. The officer promised to take my father and me to Alma-Ata for a few days.

He kept his promise. He and his driver came to town one day to pick us up for the 150-kilometers drive to the capital city, Alma-Ata. The car was beautiful, but the trip through the steppes—the vast plains of the region—was very arduous. There were no roads; we drove entirely on sand until we reached the outskirts of the city. The chauffer placed two wooden boards under the tires whenever the car's wheels lodged in the sand, which was often.

The trip took a whole day, but being in a city, even one as unimpressive and unattractive as Alma-Ata, was worth it. The officer put us up in a Russian woman's home and gave us tickets for a ballet and an opera.

The theater, made of white marble and lined with red carpeting, was stunning. There wasn't an empty seat in the house. Everyone was dressed elegantly for the occasion, except me. I had one dress to my name, the same *shmata* that I wore each day in Sary-Ozek when collecting *sachsaul*. I had no choice but to wear that dress to the theater.

Our host lent me a pair of her shoes since I had only one worn out pair. The Russian officer gave my father a pair of shoes, as well.

The ballet "Swan Lake" featured the most famous ballerina in the world at the time, Galina Ulanova. I had never seen such movements. I told the Russian officer that I didn't believe something so beautiful could exist. I was mesmerized. So was my father. We were also so impressed by the music of Tchaikovsky. The next day we attended the opera "Carmen," which was wonderful, too. After each show we returned to our host's modest farmhouse for a meal.

The Russian officer took us back to Sary-Ozek just a few days after we left. That outing was the best thing that ever happened to us since we left Dubienka. It's still hard to believe that the officer went to all of this trouble as a thank you to my father for making such a well-tailored uniform. But my father was an amazing tailor.

Two years after we arrived in Kazakhstan, news spread among the prisoners that the war had ended. It was May of 1945. I heard the news from my parents. There was no official announcement that I recall. I don't remember feeling any emotions about it. I think we were all pretty numb by that point. Was I happy to leave school? No. But I had no choice. I was never asked what I wanted. Neither were my parents.

The prisoner village guards rounded us up a couple of days after the war's end to return us to the train station, to the cattle cars that had brought us into the desert. Again, there was no explanation. My parents seemed to know we were going back to Poland. I did not understand where we were going and simply had to do as I was told. What did I know? I was just like a cattle passenger.

Chapter Five

The Aftermath of War

We left Kazakhstan in cattle cars. I don't recall how long the trip was, but I remember that I wasn't scared, despite the lack of comforts and the overwhelming uncertainty of what was to come next. I had developed a feeling of detachment over the previous hellish years. For better or worse, I learned to go with the flow—not that I had any choice in the matter.

On the train we heard stories of the concentration and extermination camps from other prisoners heading west and learned more details of the devastation and tragedy that befell millions of Jewish victims. It seemed unfathomable to me.

I felt we were likely headed back to Poland, though I had no way of knowing. If Poland was our destination, I don't believe my parents looked forward to returning.

Eventually, I saw signs along the track pointing to our final destination: Krakow. My hunch was correct. When we arrived at the station and disembarked, we heard Polish spoken publicly, which we hadn't heard in many years. We overheard Poles say to one another, with disappointment and anger, "So many Jews are still left?"

Once again, my mother knew it was time to leave. My father disagreed. "We just got here," he said. But as mentioned earlier, my mother possessed *sechel*–common sense. She probably didn't trust anyone at this point. Many of the Poles she had encountered in Dubienka, she reminded us, had accepted the Nazis' offer of a pound of sugar or a bottle of vodka to report Jews in hiding. The thought that we had to continue our journey to another unknown destination was frightening for me, but leaving Poland felt like the wise option. Little did we know then that my mother's gut feelings would again guide us out of harm's way.

I learned later that some of our fellow Jewish prisoners who chose to return to their former hometowns were severely disappointed. Their Polish neighbors in many cases had assumed ownership of their property with no intention of returning it. And in July of 1946, the townspeople of Kielce in south central Poland instigated the Kielce Pogrom that killed forty-two Jewish survivors, yet another heinous tragedy in Polish Jewish history.

In Krakow, international refugee assistance organizations were there to help us and provide information. We heard from aid workers that all the Jews from Dubienka were horrifically murdered and turned to ash. Apparently those who reported to the town center back in 1939 were sent to Majdanek, an extermination camp with gas chambers and ovens on the outskirts of Lublin. My maternal grandparents were likely among the victims. Only those who hid or fled, as we did, survived.

The refugee assistance workers told us that the closest displaced person (DP) camps were in Berlin. We had to travel west and cross the border, but we were assured that there would be assistance along the way. With their help, we boarded a train for Stettin, Poland, on the border with Germany, along with some of the people with whom we suffered in Siberia and Kazakhstan.

After the war, the Soviets claimed a significant portion of eastern Poland up to the River Bug, what is today part of Belarus and Ukraine.

Poland, in return, was given a large swath of eastern Germany. Stettin, where we were headed on the train, once belonged to Germany, but had since been handed over to postwar Poland.

When we arrived in Stettin, we found refugee assistance workers willing to help us cross into Germany. The Russian army had a significant presence at this border, on the Polish side, at least, but the border was known to be porous. Poles knew the area better than the soldiers, and knew how to sneak across.

My parents were worried that I wouldn't make it across the border with them. It was apparently a dangerous and difficult walk, plus the Russian soldiers were highly unpredictable. They made arrangements to sneak me into Germany in a mail truck. I don't recall all the details, but I did as I was told and didn't ask questions. There wasn't time. I sneaked into a box the size of a coffin and promised not to sneeze, cough or move if I heard Russian border guards during the crossing.

Inside the truck, lying in the dark, I was fearful. What would happen if I were caught? When I heard a border guard enter the truck and felt the pounding of his heavy footsteps, my heart raced. He kicked the wooden box. I tried to remain still, despite my fear. Fortunately he didn't bother to open the lid. It was a harrowing experience. The truck continued a bit further, then stopped. I reunited with my parents who crossed on foot the same day. Together we continued to Berlin.

Berlin was an absolute wreck after the war, with most buildings bombed. The city was divided into four zones by the British, French, Americans and Russians. We were taken to the British zone first, but its displaced persons (DP) camp was at capacity. They directed us to the American DP camp located in the center of Berlin. The US Army evacuated Germans from a building to create a temporary home for Jews who had escaped from Poland during the war. We knew nothing about America at that point, but were grateful when the Americans took us in, supplied us with food and shelter for a few months, and treated us like humans. It was such a relief to be treated with respect.

The American army allowed us to leave the camp and travel into the city, but we had no money, so we typically stayed in. If we ventured out it was always with a large group. We had heard that there were still many Nazis in Berlin and we could never be sure exactly who was around. I don't remember exactly how we occupied ourselves during off hours, but they gave us books to read, which kept me busy. By that time I could read Polish, Russian, Yiddish and German, so I had a lot to read.

We no longer suffered from hunger under the control of the Americans. Our food rations were limited to powdered milk and eggs with an occasional allotment of flour. Over time the supply improved to include bread, coffee, and occasionally sugar. My mother again proved her resourcefulness by concocting meals from powdered staples. Looking back, this was probably the best food for us to eat after years of such meager rations and empty stomachs.

I met many gentile German women around the camp with whom I practiced my German. I heard many of their stories from the war. There was one woman, a cook, I believe, who I spoke with on a number of occasions. She complained to me of how she struggled during the war from a lack of coffee. It was hard for me to show compassion for her "suffering."

One day the American and military policemen took all the children in camp to the circus on Friedrichstrasse, a famous street in the Russian zone of Berlin. It was so exciting. The show featured acrobatics and many animals, including elephants. In Poland, I had seen a traveling circus when I was young, but it was not nearly as good as this German one. We were even given snacks. I smiled and laughed all evening. On the way back to camp, Russian soldiers stopped our bus and demanded we show our DP camp IDs. A boy sitting in front of me presented a soldier his card. The soldier tore it up, then said, "and now what?" The Russian soldier decided for some reason or another to make this border crossing difficult. An American solider with us called his supervisor. In short time, about six American cars arrived. After prolonged negotiations over the course of a few hours, the Russians permitted our bus back into the American zone. We never returned to the circus or anywhere in the Russian part of Berlin again.

In the fall of 1945, the Americans moved us to a new DP camp in Zeilsheim, a small town in the vicinity of Frankfurt am Main, after first evacuating the local Germans. For our protection, the soldiers placed barbed wire around the entire camp while guards stood watch at the gate at all times. We quickly settled into yet another new home. Again, the Americans treated us very kindly. The soldiers assigned us various jobs to help give out the rations and maintain order within camp. Each family received a weekly ration of a pound of coffee.

I wanted to continue schooling nearby in Frankfurt, but since I had not studied in a gymnasium while imprisoned in the Russian hinterlands, I had to attain an *abitur zeugnis*—a certificate of gymnasium completion. This required taking a college entrance exam. I was well versed in Russian literature, but my German was only rudimentary, and I never studied Latin, a requirement for certification. Administers of the exam gave me books to read and recommended a German tutor in her fifties for Latin and German.

I began traveling to study at the home of my German tutor in Frankfurt. I rode in back of an American supply truck all the way to Frankfurt. I met the truck at 5 am. To return, I met the officers at a prearranged location, or I took the bus. I had no money to pay my tutor, but paid instead with my family's coffee ration, an arrangement that pleased her very much. Whenever we could spare other rations, I brought these to her, too. She demanded that I work hard. If I didn't try hard, she said, she would stop tutoring me. I began applying the same method to memorizing Latin's 500 irregular verbs that I had applied to learning poetry in Siberia: every evening I studied 15 to 20 irregular verbs at night, which would be committed to my memory when I awoke the following morning.

Even though my new instructor was strict, she turned out to be a good teacher. I was worried at first because it was so soon after the war, and she was a German gentile and I was a Polish Jew. We got along fine in the end, since we understood each other. We both had suffered and experienced loss; she lost her husband during the war and I lost my brother, as well as my childhood. With her help, I passed the exam.

I had just turned eighteen. My father felt I should pursue a profession to secure a future for myself since he had no financial assets. My mother felt that I should get married and have children and forget about becoming a professional. I sided with my father. Remembering the feeling of helplessness when my brother Joseph took ill and the many resourceful ways that my friend and mentor Galina helped so many of us survive the Gulag, I chose to become a doctor. I saw an opportunity in medicine to contribute to the world in a positive way. I had seen too much tragedy. I signed up for medical school at the Johann Wolfgang Goethe University.

While registering for school I met another young Jewish woman, a refugee from Lodz. We were the only two Jews to matriculate in medical school. Once classes began, I traveled to Frankfurt – where she lived with her husband – to study with her. She became a partner in my study group. Books were scarce those days so the University assigned students to groups. Before I had my own place, I would sleep over her apartment from time to time. It was very good to study together before exams because her husband would make us strong coffee and we'd take walks to the park to break up the monotony of studying. It was a lot of work. We both studied by ourselves, but when it came to exams, we quizzed each other. Years later, she worked as a psychiatrist in Cincinnati.

Traveling from the DP camp to Frankfurt on the back of an empty American truck became routine. I had the back of the truck all to myself since I usually caught a ride on the way to pick up provisions. The roads were in bad condition so the truck ride was bumpy, but the Americans gave me a rope to hold onto. The commute was hard, so I eventually moved into a spare room of the Jewish couple's German neighbor, a woman willing to barter my coffee ration for lodging. (Coffee was currency as good as gold in those days. You can imagine that my family never drank our coffee ration; we saved it for bartering purposes.) Without coffee, she told me, she needed daily cold compresses to treat her headaches. I returned to visit my parents at the DP camp in Zeilsheim on the weekends.

There was a young German man in my study group who took an interest in me. He was very nice and handsome. He tried to ask me out many times, but I evaded him as best I could, until one day he cornered me. "Look, I know you're avoiding me," he said, "but would you have a beer with me?" I accepted his invitation. Over drinks I tried to explain to him that the wounds the Germans had inflicted on me and my family were still very raw.

"What does this have to do with me?" he asked. "I had nothing to do with it." Even though I believed that he did not fight in the war or commit atrocities, I couldn't feel comfortable in his company. He told me his father was a pilot, and I knew all pilots in Germany were forced to be members of the SS. "You're being prejudiced," he claimed. I agreed with him, but felt I was justified. He was very kind about it, but I was nevertheless unable to date him. We remained cordial and continued to study together, but he never asked me personal questions again.

There were other reminders of Germany's evils during the war that made studying and living there a trial. Even though the German language was not challenging to learn, it was difficult to live with. I tried to concentrate on Germany's history of great music and literature. Yet when I traveled between Frankfurt and Zeilsheim, I passed the factories for Hoechst AG Farben Industrie. When I asked my German medical school colleague about it, he said, "You don't want to know." The company, I learned, was responsible for producing all the gases used in the concentration camps.

I wondered how the German people accepted Hitler, but I didn't ask Germans because most were unwilling to discuss the past. Some were too fixated on their own suffering. It was a complex situation that I just didn't fully understand. It took years for German society to come to terms with the atrocities of the Holocaust.

There were Jewish organizations that came to our camp in Zeilsheim to help refugees like us register for visas to foreign countries. We had x-rays and other medical tests performed. Some people in our DP camp opted to immigrate to Canada, some chose to register for visas to South America, but we sought visas for the United States, which was possible because of my father's sister in New York. It was the only place we wanted to go. We didn't know what awaited us, but we figured it couldn't be any worse than Europe.

I was starting my second year of medical school when my mother told me she was pregnant. After my parents lost their son, I didn't think they wanted to have another child, but I never inquired about their motivations. More than a year after moving to Zeilsheim, my sister was born. Her name was Bluma. She later adopted the name Frances, but we called her Franny. It was April 10th, 1947. At first I was embarrassed to be a mature woman with a baby sister. Then I adapted to the fact and did my best to be nice to her any way I could.

We remained in that camp until the summer of 1949, when we officially received a visa from the American consulate. It took two years for the visa to process. We had been in Zeilsheim for three. Once we received our visas, we were ready to leave. There wasn't much to pack, so I just had to notify the university of my plans. I received a certificate listing the coursework I had completed, so hopefully I could continue my studies in America – not knowing what lay ahead in the "land of the free." We made our plans for yet one more journey, this time with Franny, my new baby sister.

Chapter Six

Freedom in the New World

In 1949 we left for the United States. The trip was quite arduous. We traveled from Zeilsheim to Bremerhaven, a German port city on the North Sea about 500 kilometers from Frankfurt. We boarded an American naval ship by the name of General W.G. Haan on December 18, 1949 leaving Bremerhaven. We spent ten long days on that shaky old ship packed to the brim with mostly Polish refugees seeking a new life in America. Most passengers were grateful to be aboard. We were given food and it wasn't very good, but it was at least edible. We slept on bunk beds. It was like a new world, so much better than what we had grown accustomed to in Europe. It wasn't quite the Queen Mary, but we were glad to be heading to the United States. We were fortunate that my father's sister agreed to sponsor us.

Throughout the voyage, sailors painted the ship. Each day they added fresh layers of blue and white paint. The fumes, combined with choppy waters, made me seasick. I spent most of my time onboard nauseated, so I couldn't eat much. I tried to remain positive. I'll never forget how all the passengers applauded when we could see the Statue of Liberty. We shed tears of joy. The statue symbolized an end to the horrific years we faced in Europe due to the Holocaust. It also meant that my nausea would soon end.

After 10 days, we arrived at Ellis Island on December 28, 1949. We disembarked in an orderly fashion. An agent registered my parents, my sister Franny, and me. Franny was just two-years-old. The agent couldn't spell my father's family name, Nuwendstern, so he changed it to Newton. He also changed his first name from Pincus to the more American-sounding Paul, and mine from Cyla to the more Anglicized Celia. We became Paul and Celia Newton. But my mother remained Ita because her name was easier to spell. The agents asked us additional questions, and then dismissed us. Before we left Ellis Island, we registered with HIAS, the Hebrew Immigrant Aid Society, which helped transition Jewish immigrants to life in the United States. We had an appointment to visit their offices in Manhattan the next day.

Anna Stelnik, my father's older sister, came by car with her husband to pick us up in Manhattan. The U.S. consulate in Germany helped track her down to secure our visa. My father's reunion with his sister was a very exciting moment, but also an awkward one. They didn't remember one another; my father hadn't seen her since he was still a child. The immigration agents introduced them as if they were complete strangers. The two hugged. Anna then welcomed our whole family to the United States and brought us to her home in Brooklyn. She cooked for us and seemed very happy to see us and take care of us for a short period, but we had to work to get to know one another. And though Anna mainly spoke English and our family Yiddish, we sat and talked for a while in our broken languages. Over time, we all developed a relationship with each other, and Anna proved indispensable in the transition to our new life.

The day after our arrival, Anna took us to HIAS's Manhattan office for an extensive interview. The HIAS representatives offered us money and help finding an apartment. My father refused the money. He was a very proud, hard-working man. He asked if they could help him find work instead. They agreed. In a very short period of time HIAS found us an apartment on 125th Street and Madison Avenue. Soon thereafter, my parents enrolled Franny in pre-school.

HIAS found my father a job as a tailor in a garment factory, but very quickly the factory supervisors noticed that he was a qualified tailor and suggested that he work for a designer, which he promptly did. My father's supervisors were very pleased with his work, but after a while my father felt that he wasn't being paid well enough for the work he was providing. He felt exploited.

A year or so later, as my father's English improved, he opened his own tailor and dry cleaning store on West 96th Street between Broadway and Amsterdam, and found an apartment on the same street, at 110 West 96th Street. It was a new learning experience. He paid taxes and kept the books. My mother had a better business sense than him. She worked at the register and handled the dry cleaning portion of the business while he focused on the tailoring. My father felt much better working for himself. He never became rich, but he was always able to support himself and the family. He liked the work, too. As usual, his attention to detail was impeccable. People in the neighborhood were delighted to have such a good tailor who treated everyone fairly, which kept him very busy. Together my parents became very popular shopkeepers in the neighborhood.

New York was so different from the other cities I'd known and far more overwhelming. I felt freedom for the first time in my life. We didn't even need an ID to apply for a job or to open a store or to travel. We were happy to be there, even though we quickly realized it was an expensive city. Shopping was actually quite challenging and confusing for us. I remember my mother and I just standing in an aisle in the supermarket staring at all of the options. We had never seen so much variety. Aunt

Anna eventually showed us how to go to a store and compare prices. She was very helpful. We learned quickly.

Initially my parents didn't get involved with a synagogue since they were so busy settling into New York life. There was too much to do that first year. But that changed when they moved to 96th Street. It was mostly my mother's idea. They attended Shabbat services regularly at Congregation Ohab Zedek, a synagogue on West 95th Street.

Once my parents settled into the city, my mother returned to cooking foods from Dubienka, like chicken soup and kreplach for Shabbat dinner, and other specialties such as potato pierogi and cheese blintzes for the week. My mother's cooking was wonderful. She kept a kosher home, only bought kosher meat and always made the most delicious food. And for the first time in her life she owned a refrigerator, which made her happy.

On Sundays, the whole family accompanied my father to the Lower East Side to pick up the fabrics and garments he needed for his business. In his spare time—which was rare until his retirement years later—he made clothing for my mother, my sister and me. I still wear some of the most beautiful evening dresses, coats and suits that he made.

I really enjoyed the Lower East Side at the time. I felt at home on its streets with the foods that I remembered from Poland, including blintzes, knishes, bagels and more, all over the neighborhood. Sometimes we'd have lunch at Grand Dairy Restaurant, a quiet restaurant on Grand Street between Essex and Ludlow with good soups and sandwiches. We went to Katz's Delicatessen on Houston Street once in a while, but my mother developed diabetes and she couldn't tolerate such heavy meat dishes.

I maintained a close relationship with the lady who sold us bagels and pletzlach on Grand Street near the fabric shops. She liked me. "Take one," she would say, "these just came out of the oven." She didn't charge me. We talked with each other on my trips with my father. Once I told her I wanted to go back to medical school and she told me that two of her sons were studying medicine.

I began to feel lost in America. Franny was signed up for school, my father returned to his profession as a tailor and my mother worked with him and took care of things at home. Yet I was stuck between adolescence and adulthood. I was very pleased to be in the United States where there was a possibility that I could become a citizen. The United States had a reputation for being more accepting of refugees than elsewhere. But citizenship wasn't enough. I had to figure out what I wanted from my life. My parents weren't able to emotionally support me at this point. It was during this period of unrest that returning to medical school to finish my degree became a priority. I had left a degree unfinished, and pursuing my medical profession, I hoped, would give me purpose. First, I needed to be able to speak English well enough for my interview. But I couldn't go to school to learn English because I had no money to do so. So I studied the language however I could: listening to the radio, speaking with Americans and reading *The New York Times* like my father. At first he only read the Yiddish *Forward* newspaper, but it was surprisingly hard for him to understand, since too often English words were written out in Yiddish characters.

I went looking for a job in medicine to bolster my resume. I looked up hospitals in the phone book and found a listing for Beth David Hospital on the Upper East Side. I walked along on the park side of Fifth Avenue toward the hospital to apply. That's when I saw an elegant-looking gentleman pass by. I stopped him to ask where Beth David was located. "Why do you want to know?" he asked.

"I'm looking to work while I apply to medical school," I explained. "I need experience in a laboratory."

The elegant man turned out to be Dr. Gudeman, the director of the laboratory at Beth David Hospital. It was a fortuitous meeting because he was looking to temporarily replace his lab technician, who had requested to travel for the summer. His technician, an older Russian woman, made it difficult to replace her. She didn't label any bottles in the lab, so only she knew what each bottle contained. I accepted the job, and since I spoke Russian, I agreed to train for a period with her. One evening, I worked in the lab with the technician well into midnight, speaking in Russian, labeling each bottle while I learned how to perform the necessary tests.

The Beth David Hospital soon shut down, forcing me to look for another job. I applied to work at Mount Sinai with Dr. Isidore Snapper, the Director of Medicine at the hospital with an interest in bone metabolism. I also found a side job with Dr. Charkov, an American professor of medicine who studied Russian in his spare time. Dr. Charkove paid me to meet him once a week to converse in Russian for an hour. He told me that I helped him improve his conversational language skills. I was embarrassed to take money from him because I enjoyed our time together so much. Dr. Charkov also recommended me to the Academy of Medicine. A friend of his there didn't care to read whole articles about neurology in Russian, so I read them and wrote abstracts in English.

By that time I had quite a few friends in New York, including Bianca Schneid, a Viennese refugee who ran Dr. Snapper's laboratory, and Mira, a Polish Jewish woman who worked as a technician with me. All of these new contacts were very helpful.

I let myself get comfortable in New York. In time, Mira set me up with a friend of her husband's, a young American man who worked as a physicist. It was very nice to spend time with him. He was intelligent. We went around New York together, to museums and restaurants, and he took me the opera and the theater. We only saw musicals like *Annie*

Get Your Gun because I didn't know enough English to see dramatic theater, or so he believed. He was very considerate. We spoke together in English, which was very good for my language skills. He claimed to be in love with me.

I looked into the possibility of attending medical school in the United States. It looked bleak. I met young Jewish Americans who couldn't get accepted to programs in the country. I spoke with the doctors I knew.

"Dear child," Dr. Snapper said to me, "you are poor, you are a refugee, you are a woman and you are Jewish. You will not get into medical school in this country." Not to mention that my English was hardly fluent. It became obvious that there was little chance that I would be accepted into an American medical school. I liked New York very much and would have liked to stay, but it seemed hopeless.

I learned that European schools were open to admitting foreigners. I didn't want to return to Germany because of too many unpleasant memories. The universities of Switzerland, I had heard, survived the war intact, unlike in the rest of Europe. Since I was fluent in German and didn't know much French, I applied to schools in Bern, Basel and Zurich, Switzerland's three German speaking medical schools. Bern responded promptly with an acceptance, contingent on proving to the Swiss government that I wouldn't be a financial burden. I asked Mr. Schwartz, a distant relative of mine with a factory in New York, to be my guarantor. He agreed.

I also needed to prove that I could support myself in Switzerland and to pay for school. My parents were new immigrants and could scarcely keep the family afloat. I went to the New York Public Library at 42nd Street to look up scholarship opportunities. I discovered a foundation that provided educational scholarships for Jewish women. I applied. In a few weeks, I had an appointment to meet with a member of the foundation. I sat down with the wife of an obstetrician at her home on

Park Avenue. I was in awe of her beautiful house. When I arrived, she was sitting in the living room and sewing labels onto children's clothing. While she interviewed me, she explained, she would have to continue sewing labels, since the kids were leaving for camp the next day. "If you supply me with needle and thread," I offered, "I can help you." We sewed together while I answered questions about where I'm from, how I survived the war, what I have in the way of family, and the type of education I received in Europe. I showed her my acceptance letter from Bern and explained that I started my medical education in the DP camp. After an hour and a half, she was impressed.

"I would like to help you," she said, "but we have never given a scholarship to a student who plans to study in a foreign country." I told her that maybe if I apply for a partial scholarship and a partial loan, the committee might feel more secure investing in me. She offered to propose it to the board. We said our farewells and I returned home. A few weeks later, my request was approved with the condition that once a year a representative will travel to Bern to check up on me. If I was a good student and if I performed exactly as expected, the scholarship funds would continue. Each year a representative did visit to check on my status as a student. I was not worried, since from the start I intended to do my best in school.

I had many misgivings about moving so far away, leaving my family and my new life behind to go back to Europe, to a country that I knew little about. Where would I live? What if I don't know enough? Was it the correct decision? When you survive a war with a small family and you plan to leave them for a number of years, you have to be serious about your intentions.

My parents were sorry to let me go, but they realized it was what I wanted. My father was pleased that I was pursuing a profession. My mother, on the other hand, liked the man I was dating. She wanted me to marry him and stay in the United States. He had told me he loved me. When I told him that I had to go away to finish medical school, his love for me seemed to evaporate. Our relationship of a few months ended when I left for school. While I liked him, I wasn't in love.

By the end of August in 1950 I had received my green card, in addition to a single entry visa into Switzerland. I was off to my next adventure.

Chapter Seven

Back to Europe

I left my new life in New York to return to Europe. I boarded the Queen Mary, a beautiful British passenger cruiser heading to Bremen, Germany, a northern port city. I couldn't afford the elegant first class accommodations, so I bunked in the base of the ship for the five-day journey. I shared a bunk bed with an Italian girl about my age who told me she was part of the famous Fiat family. Whether or not that was true, she was very lovely and an experienced traveler, so she helped me through my disorientation. She also taught me when to go to the dining room to avoid the kippers—fried herring—whose smell I found repugnant. When I arrived in Bremen, I quickly made my way to the train station to board a train for half day's journey to Bern, the capital of Switzerland.

Bern was a very attractive city, clearly untouched by the war. Well-maintained cobblestone roads lined the city center, where covered archways created shadows on the streets and clock towers called *zeitglocken* kept precise time. There were museums and theaters, and even a famous bear pit where bears lived in a hole in the ground for passersby to observe them. (The bear pit, connected to a park for them to roam, is called Barengraben and still exists today.) Mountains surrounded the entire city and the Aare River majestically flowed through its center. Several bridges spanned the river's banks. Bern appeared prosperous with its great cafes and restaurants. When I walked into the Migros market, one of the several premiere supermarkets, there was an entire wall of chocolates. I had never seen such a sight. A salesperson saw me staring in disbelief and asked if he could be of any help. Overall, people were friendly and polite, yet distant and detached. I lived there for two years before a fellow Swiss student finally invited me to tea. It took another two years to receive an invitation to the home of my professor.

Once I arrived, I headed straight to the University of Bern to register with the medical school. But before classes began I was in need of an apartment. I went to a café, ordered a coffee and asked the waitress the best way to find a modest lodging. She brought me the local ad paper, *Tages-Anzeiger*, where I saw a listing for a room and bath for sublet by a widow named Frau Sutter who was looking for a student. I took the trolley to Hallerstrasse 62 with my luggage. After a brief conversation, I moved in.

Frau Sutter was a very polite landlord, but she was incredibly stingy with heat in wintertime. Rather than turn up the heat, each night she brought me a hot water bottle for my feet. She was a very depressed and particularly nosy woman. She read the *Tages-Anzeiger* every day, not for the news reports but to keep tabs on local families. "If the Josephs sell their baby carriage," she once told me, "that means they won't have any more children. And if this photographer sells his equipment it means he no longer wants to be a photographer."

The medical school was comprised of various departmental buildings sprawled around one large campus. Once classes began, I spent a lot of time walking from lecture to lecture. I started very early—at eight a.m. in the winter and seven a.m. in the spring. I was on a tight budget, so I always went home for lunch.

Initially we studied physiology, anatomy and biochemistry, then we moved on to bacteriology, medicine, pediatrics, surgery, pharmacology, radiology and social sciences. The professors I encountered in Switzerland were very smart. It was a pleasure to listen to Professor Abelin's lectures on chemistry. I also had a professor of surgery who was particularly demanding. He placed a sign on top of the blackboard that read: "May God protect me from all evil and from becoming an interesting patient." To be "interesting" as a patient meant doctors didn't know what was wrong. Our professors encouraged us to study subjects outside of medicine, like philosophy, which I knew nothing about. The very first philosopher I studied was Nietzsche. It was hard to figure out what he was saying.

My first six months in school were depressing even though I loved to learn. I went to class, returned home, studied, and then returned to school the next day. The rote memorization for my histology, anatomy and physiology courses in the early years of school drove me crazy. If we didn't study each day, we could never really memorize verbatim what we were taught and also understand it all. I had to work very hard to keep up. I felt very lonely.

I missed my parents terribly. I mostly wore clothes that my father tailored just for me, so I thought of him almost everyday. I wrote a letter to him expressing my misgivings about school. "Maybe I made a mistake in leaving New York?" I wrote. He reassured me: "Put up with your first year, and if you continue to feel the same way, we can revisit the issue." He reminded me how important it is for me to have a profession. Then he asked, "Why did you think it would be easy?"

Throughout my difficult time at school, I made sure to remind myself what made Galina from the Gulag such a good doctor. She wasn't simply erudite; her social skills and her ability to connect with people made her exceptional. My mother once said, "If you want to learn medicine, you go to school—but it's character you bring from home. It's not something they teach in school."

Despite the hard work, I managed to receive high grades. I also developed good study habits, unlike the Americans, who were in for a rude awakening. The Americans initially mimicked the Swiss students, who were seen sitting around coffee shops, cycling around town and leaving for ski weekends. But they never saw the Swiss students studying in private, so when it came time for our first anatomy exam, all the Americans failed. The anatomy professor, a rigid but decent man, said, "You're foreigners and the language is new, so I'll give you one more chance." The Americans soon got their act together.

All in all, there were about fifteen Jewish American students in my class. There were about 80 Jewish American students at school in Geneva, Zurich or Bern altogether. Most of them were not admitted to American medical schools. I was a curiosity to them. While I came from the U.S., my English was poor and my German was far better than any of theirs. I was better able to understand the professors and take good notes. I was also the only woman among the Jewish students.

My time in Bern took a turn for the better as I connected to the Jewish community in the city. Somebody told me that there was a friendly congregation in town. I attended services at the synagogue and met new friends who were originally from Poland. I appreciated meeting people who understood my background. Eventually I moved from Frau Sutter's apartment to a room with a Jewish family, which was much closer to school. I could walk to class instead of taking two trollies. My new landlords were originally from the town of Lvov in Southeastern Poland. They had purchased a second home in Bern before the war. Once Hitler invaded Poland, they fled to their second home. Jews were not permitted entry into Switzerland then, unless they owned property, which is how they made it through.

My friend from the Jewish community, Frau Rotterberg, had a son who was studying physics at the University. She showed me how to make very good apple strudel. She would roll out the dough on a tablecloth and place apples, cinnamon, sugar and raisins on it. She would then lift the tablecloth and roll the dough, wrapping in the filling, then transfer it straight into a baking pan. I still follow her recipe.

My scholarship covered about 20% of the costs of school and the Swiss government covered the rest. Since I had received a loan and scholarship from the Educational Foundation for Jewish Girls, I paid nothing. I had a dollar a day for spending after I paid my rent and commuting fares. One dollar then was four and a half Swiss Francs. (A loaf of bread and a Lindt chocolate both cost only one Franc each.) With my stipend, I never went hungry. I cooked at home, almost always. Additionally, my parents sent me a bit of extra spending money and clothing made by my father, including a custom-made parka with wool and fake fur lining (so it could be washed), which kept me very warm come wintertime.

As per my arrangement with the Educational Foundation for Jewish Girls, the organization sent a representative with her husband to check up on me. In fact, each year for four years in a row, a new woman was sent to visit me in Switzerland. I provided my sponsors with the names of my professors for them to question. My guests usually wanted to shop for fine china while visiting. I joined them and translated along the way. Each year I was treated to the best restaurant in town, or at least the restaurant that I suggested was the best. Of course I never ate in such restaurants alone, but I knew which ones were well regarded. The first year I took my guests to Hermitage, a typical fine Swiss restaurant. My guests were nervous about hygiene in postwar Europe so they only ordered from a limited menu to avoid raw vegetables. They didn't seem to understand that unlike the rest of Europe, Switzerland did not suffer through the war and hadn't undergone any food shortages. I decided to have as good a meal as possible in their company. I ate a lot. My healthy appetite surprised them. All in all, my sponsors' visits were pleasant. They reported that I was a good student, so my funding continued.

Summertime in Bern was very pleasant and nice. I missed July and August there each year in order to travel to the United States and visit with my parents, work at various hospital labs and, most important, register my green card each year as a student. But May and June were beautiful months to spend in Bern and its surrounding region. Sometimes in the spring, snow remained in the mountains. Crocus flowers bloomed beside the snow. It was stunning. On weekends most students went hiking. I saved up for a pair of Bally hiking boots for a whole year. When I wore my brand new boots to an organized hike, the guide wouldn't let me continue. Break them in first, he told me. It was his policy.

As part of medical school, my Swiss friend Anna Marie and I were assigned to bring rural Swiss men and women in to our medical school's clinic, since they were developing abscesses from exposure to tubercular cows. We stayed in country folks' primitive homes in the mountains, which were more like mountain chalets with two beds for caretakers and some space for cows to graze. We stayed overnight, then moved on to the next village in the morning. Anna Marie taught me the Bernese dialect of German (each county had its own). Most countryside folks made their own potions and ointments at home and didn't trust doctors. Convincing them to come down to the clinic was like trying to move mountains. The government eventually replaced each sick cow with two healthy cows to handle the epidemic.

Bern was in the mountains, so there was a lot of snow. In February each year, there was a week when students from around the country all descended upon the Palace Hotel in Davos for a special student rate of just one hundred dollars for the entire week. The deal included a room, breakfast, packed lunch, dinner, and a free pass on all Alpine trails and lifts, as well as discounted train fare to Davos and to the glaciers on the other side of the ski town. The entire hotel was filled with students.

All my colleagues were expert skiers. I was not. I rented skis and shoes and joined a group of five-year-olds on an *idioten hugel*—idiot's hill. During the first lesson I learned how to accelerate, stop and fall. When I fell, the kids laughed at me. I never became an expert but I could negotiate part of the mountain in Davos. I would ski to the middle stop and then take the ski lift downhill the rest of the way.

One time at the middle stop, one of my Swiss colleagues suggested that I sled the rest of the way down a track of ice. I don't know why, but I listened to him and lay down headfirst on the sled, which traveled at breakneck speed, hitting wall after wall of ice along the way. Upset, I later asked him why he put me in harm's way. "Now you will have something to tell your grandchildren," he said. The following year that same colleague hit a tree while skiing. I visited him in the Davos hospital when he was in critical condition. He did not make it in the end.

In my second year of medical school, friends of mine introduced me to a young man named Richard Ores because we were both survivors from Poland. Richard was two years ahead of me, though eight years my senior. I found him to be very charming. He was also incredibly bright. We bumped into each other often and felt comfortable speaking Polish with one another. I learned a bit about him and his family. He was very proud to have been born in Krakow. He teased me for being from a *shtetl*

even though by the time I arrived in Switzerland I had traveled halfway around the world and back again.

Richard spoke often of his family. His parents Oscar and Pauline Ores, and his sister Antonina were unfortunately all killed in Belzec, an extermination camp near Krakow. His only living relative was his mother's brother, Max Gartenberg, who lived with his wife Stasia in Montreal. He told me how his mother had come from the line of Gartenbergs who were very well known in Poland.

After the Krakow Ghetto, Richard survived several concentration camps, including Plaszow and Auschwitz. He was liberated in Dachau. After the war, he was diagnosed with tuberculosis and shipped to the Davos Sanitarium in Switzerland. He beat the disease by drinking pickle juice, he claimed, which he said contained streptomycin. Then he received a scholarship to University of Bern Medical School.

Towards the end of my second year, Richard invited me to go dancing on a Saturday night at the local dance hall. We were both poor, but buying a single bottle of wine allowed us to dance all evening. He told me I was a good dancer. It just so happens that I loved to dance. My hearing was impeccable so I could follow the music's rhythm perfectly. At end of school each year there was always a big elegant ball, for which my father sent me a pale green evening dress. Men wanted to dance with me because I wouldn't step on their feet.

Soon Richard and I spent more time together when we were not in class, and began picnicking, hiking and skiing together. He took me on excursions to Swiss cities such as Ronco and Lugano, and boat rides on Lago Maggiore. I recall that our trip to Lago Maggiore on the border of Italy and Switzerland was particularly harrowing. We took a boat to visit islands on the lake but without realizing that we had crossed into Italy. When we turned the boat around, border guards did not permit my re-entry to Switzerland. My visa was single entry. After several hours I convinced the border agents to call the Bern police, who knew all the foreigners in town. The police verified I was a student and said that I could leave if I promised to head to the American consulate.

I thoroughly enjoyed my time with Richard. Every Saturday we went dancing together and I fell in love. In a short time, he expressed his desire to marry me. He told me he envied people with families, and since he lost his in the war, he was eager to start anew. I liked him very much, but the whole thing happened so fast. Towards the end of my third year, about a year after we first went dancing, we were engaged.

Getting married was not as easy as we had thought. Planning a wedding was complicated since we were both stateless. He was not able to come to the United States until I received citizenship. The Swiss did not want to marry us unless we could produce birth certificates, which we could not do, because of the war.

Menek Goldstein, a friend of ours from medical school – originally from an Orthodox family in Poland – had an idea. An Orthodox rabbi could not refuse to marry us, he said, otherwise we would "live in sin," for which the rabbi would take the blame.

Menek had an aunt in Zurich where there was an Orthodox Jewish community. She arranged for us to meet with the rabbi. I spent the remainder of my money to have my hair done and to buy a hat in Bern. My father sent me a navy suit he had tailored for the occasion. Off we went. The rabbi was not too anxious to perform the rites, but he acquiesced as long as I dunked my whole body in the *mikveh*. I agreed. The money I spent on my hairdo went to waste. We proceeded to the synagogue where we were married in a very small ceremony. Religious marriages were not accepted by the Swiss, so from Zurich we journeyed to London where we found an international lawyer who, on the basis of our religious marriage, arranged for a civil ceremony in Caxton Hall. The date was June 30th, 1954. After all this, we were legally married.

When we returned to Bern we moved in together to an apartment on 42 Buhlstrasse. Richard, since he had already graduated, enrolled in the Faculty of Chemistry at the University. By the next summer, at the end of my fourth year of school, I was pregnant. I sailed to New York on an American ship in the last month of pregnancy. I chose an American ship so that if I went into labor onboard, the ship would have been considered American territory. I traveled to the U.S. to contact my Congressman to obtain my citizenship and secure Richard a visa, so the baby would have no citizenship issues.

I traveled third class, but when the captain found out that I was a student, he invited me to dinner at his first class dining table. I was seated next to the ship's doctor who drank three martinis during the cocktail hour alone. I was petrified that if I went into labor onboard, this man would be completely useless. When I returned to my cabin, I told the Irish caretaker of the cabin that I could not trust the doctor. He told me not to worry– he delivered all five of his children himself.

I made it to the states without going into labor, then began my travels to Washington D.C. to my Congressman. After waiting, I was able to obtain a letter that expedited my citizenship process. The Congressman asked that a visa be granted to Richard since we were expecting a baby. Richard met me in the U.S. once his visa was issued and he could travel.

I delivered my daughter in January 1955 at Mount Sinai Hospital. Dr. Novak delivered her. The birth was painful, but it was wonderful to bring a child into this world. We named her Pauline, after Richard's mother. I loved her. I received a number of presents and toys from family and friends during the week and a half we stayed in the United States.

We headed back to our one-bedroom apartment in Bern with Pauline. She slept in the living room since we had no other space, and played with pot and pans, which she seemed to prefer to her toys. In order to return to school, we hired a young girl to look after her during the day.

Initially medical school was very difficult as a new mother, but then I developed a system: I put her to sleep early, studied, then woke up early and studied more. I worked very hard despite the new responsibilities, because I had to maintain high grades to stay on scholarship.

When Dr. Isidore Snapper—whose bone metabolism lab I worked for over several summers in New York—was promoted to Director of Medicine in Brooklyn at the Brookdale Medical Center, he wrote me a letter saying that he would welcome both me and Richard for internship after medical school. The hospital provided housing and we could eat in the cafeteria for free. Our salary would be just $100 each per month. It was an amazing opportunity and one that allowed us to plan our family's return to New York.

As we wrapped up school and our lives in Bern, I met a waitress in a restaurant who wanted to move to the United States. Her name was Bertha Bucheli and we got along well. I invited her to join us to look after Pauline, as long as she stayed for one year and agreed to what we could pay her, which was only $100 per month. She would find out quickly that she was underpaid. She nevertheless agreed, and in the spring of 1956 our new family boarded a boat for the United States, leaving behind the beautiful city of mountains and cobblestone streets where we all first came together.

Chapter 8

New York City: Work and Family

Richard, Pauline, Berta and I took up residence in a modest, second floor apartment in a two-family attached house provided by the Brookdale Hospital in Flatbush, Brooklyn. We were both beginning our two-year internships with Dr. Isidore Snapper. I would later intern with Dr. Bella Shick in Pediatrics (well known for inventing the diphtheria vaccine) who was also at Brookdale.

My parents were incredibly happy to have me back in New York City. They were proud that I made it through medical school and delighted to have a granddaughter. When I could, I traveled to the Upper West Side of Manhattan to visit them and my sister at their apartment at 110 West 96th Street, right across from my father's tailor shop. They visited us often and offered to help out however they could and even gave us Pauline's first baby carriage. They were so good with her. I can't imagine those early years of motherhood without their support.

Brooklyn was certainly a long way from Bern. There were no mountains to hike or elegant bridges to walk over. My return to the United States was so defined by work and family obligations that I don't believe I would have had the time to appreciate the beauty around me had I lived somewhere more scenic. The transition from a student's life with flexible hours to a doctor's life with endless work shifts was extremely challenging, especially as a new mother. I was constantly tired. I slept in scrubs in anticipation of calls to return to the hospital in the middle of the night. Looking back, the whole medical system that keeps young doctors awake for endless shifts seems ridiculous.

I worked hard to adjust to American attitudes and protocols, conversational English, as well as new procedures and equipment, but I really knew my medicine. It helped that Dr. Snapper was a good teacher with high expectations for his interns. Each week he conducted "grand rounds," during which he presented a group of interns with complicated cases. He encouraged us to think out diagnoses. Most of the time our hunches were incorrect, but slowly we improved.

There was camaraderie among the residents, which I really cherished. We all went out of our way to help each other. When interns were assigned patients who only spoke German or Yiddish (quite commonly spoken in Jewish neighborhoods), they traded with me for English-speaking patients. That same year, I took postgraduate courses at New York University to improve my English.

Balancing work, language studies and parenthood would have been all but impossible without Berta, our Swiss nanny. She was remarkable. I could go to work all day (sometimes at night) and not worry about Pauline's care. Despite only a grade school education, Berta was unbelievably smart. I signed her up for English classes and within six months she spoke fluently. She learned faster than me.

At a hundred dollars a month—what we had agreed to pay Berta in Switzerland and precisely my salary as an intern—she was a real bargain. Her aunt, for the sake of comparison, earned her monthly salary in a few days of tips as a waitress at Rumpelmayer's Tea and Pastry Café in the well-known Hotel St. Moritz on Central Park South. Berta had nevertheless committed to stay for one year and wound up staying for two and a half. She eventually moved to Chicago to marry Hans Giovanoli, a Swiss man from Engadin, a long valley in Southeastern Switzerland (part of the Alps), who was teaching hotelier cooking.

Losing Berta was difficult; she had become a confidante. I wanted to help her succeed in Chicago so I called Dr. Novak, the daughter of my obstetrician and by then a well-established pathologist in Chicago, and told her that she simply must hire Berta. "I would hold on to her for dear life if I could," I told her. Luckily, Dr. Novak listened to me. Within three months she called to tell me that the histology slides Berta arranged were perfectly organized. She sent her to train as a histology technician; in less than a year Berta was overseeing twelve technicians and was in charge of the laboratory. A few years later Berta and her husband Hans moved to Eureka, CA, a fishing village just north of San Francisco where they remain to this day. They opened a bakery there and specialized in Swiss cakes, breads and cookies. (We've stayed in touch over the years, and incidentally, I just went to visit them for the first time in 2014 with my granddaughter Lia. They treated us wonderfully and it was such a pleasure to see her again.)

About two years after moving to Brooklyn, I learned I was pregnant again. I was elated, but also nervous. As a pediatric resident, I understood the challenges of childbirth firsthand and knew complications were all too common. Luckily, David was born without incident in January 1958. Berta was looking after Pauline when I went into labor. My parents joined me at the hospital to greet my new baby and me. Their dedication lifted my spirits. David was alert, active and the cutest thing on earth. He was so special from early on. Three years later Michelle was born in November 1961. It was another blessing.

My children brought me so much joy. They were absolutely wonderful. You should have seen how handsome David was at age two. He was remarkably active and bright. Pauline was incredibly well behaved and helpful. And Michelle was so lively and friendly.

When our Brookdale internships ended that same year, Richard accepted a residency at Columbia Presbyterian Hospital in neurology to study electron microscopy with Dr. Leon Roizin. Columbia was far from Brookdale, so to be close to my husband, I applied to a pediatric residency at Babies Hospital, now known as the Morgan Stanley Children's Hospital at Columbia Presbyterian. I traveled to Washington Heights to interview with Dr. Dorothy Andersen, a leading researcher of Cystic Fibrosis (CF) at Babies Hospital and a relative of the famous writer, Hans Christian Andersen. Dr. Andersen impressed me right away. We sat and talked with ease for about an hour. That same day she sent me for a second interview with Dr. Rusty McIntosh, her superior. It was clear by the second interview that Dorothy's influence would be enough to ensure my hire and, in due time, I started a residency at Babies Hospital—the beginning of what would become a long career at Columbia.

With a larger family and residencies at Columbia in Northern Manhattan, Richard and I looked for a closer home with more space. Many Columbia faculty members - including Dr. Andersen–lived in Leonia, New Jersey, just across the George Washington Bridge, so we followed their lead. Richard found a house at 254 Christie Heights Street, right across the street from the town's high school. We moved from the city in the winter of 1961, just after Michelle was born.

Leonia was a great place to raise a family. I spent as much time with my three children as I could, given my demanding schedule. I read stories to them at night and ensured good food was always on the table. I made sure they were on top of their homework and I attended school meetings and performances when I could.

Dr. Andersen, who I called Dr. Dorothy, became my mentor for many years. She also became a good friend. She would visit our house and bring books for the children. She was also the only colleague with whom I shared the details of my past. When she first interviewed me for the job, she asked where I was from. I explained to her how I came from Eastern Poland, then was sent to Siberia and Kazakhstan, eventually moved to Germany, and finally settled in the U.S. When I came back from Switzerland with a medical degree, there were many stumbling blocks for people who came from European schools, so naturally I was a bit wary. Yet Dorothy understood me in a way no one else did. Dr. McIntosh eventually found out about my past because he asked me direct questions, but typically I didn't explain my experience during the Holocaust. There were only a handful of Jews in pediatrics at Columbia at the time, and there weren't many survivors in professional life at all. Most survivors went into business or took jobs like my father had done.

Not long after moving to Leonia I found myself pregnant again. I gained a lot of weight—up to 40 pounds. In previous pregnancies I had gained only 20. This time my body felt a bit different. When I walked, I waddled like a duck. My doctor, Dr. Todd, told me not to worry, but I sensed there was a problem when he kept details about my condition from me. I asked another doctor who told me that there was a complication: apparently a diaphragmatic hernia interfered with the circulation of vital organs in my body. I decided to carry the pregnancy to term since there was little else I could do.

When I felt labor pains, I drove to Columbia Presbyterian. Dr. Todd met me there, but again, frustratingly, said nothing. I gave birth that day to a baby boy in distress. I named him Michael. The nurses transferred him immediately to the ICU where Dr. Phillip Wiedel operated on him. Despite the hospital's excellent care and Dr. Wiedel's kindness, Michael only lived for a few days. We had a small funeral. To this day, I can't visit his grave. It makes me too sad.

After Michael's death, it became clear that after 13 years of marriage, Richard and I were not going to make it. He was not a committed father or a true partner in marriage. We divorced shortly afterwards in 1967 and hardly spoke again. He continued to see the children once a week but that was about it. I received no court mandated alimony payments after the first couple of weeks, but I did keep the house and full custody of the children. My marriage was very difficult for me and I was solely responsible for the children, work and the home. But the divorce was difficult, too.

My parents, after closing their tailor shop on West 96th Street in about 1970, eventually moved to Fort Lee, New Jersey to be close by and to help me with Pauline, David and Michelle, which I desperately needed. My mother and father visited daily at around three in the afternoon and stayed with the children until I came home from work. My mother cooked pierogi, cheese blintzes and other Polish snacks for the kids. We dedicated a room for my father's tailoring so he could get some work done while my mother looked after the children.

The period after the divorce was a very difficult time of my life, but I continued to work and raise the children and push ahead. I did not talk about the divorce much because it was a taboo subject at the time. Divorce was not common until the early 1970s, so that made my situation all that much more lonely and difficult. Now, in retrospect, I can see how Richard's leaving me made me a stronger person. I put up with a lot of garbage from him, because he had a type of character that no amount of good will or attention could change.

Fortunately, I had my children. They kept me strong and gave me purpose. The kids were all very active, too, and loved animals. We had two Bernese Mountain Dogs named Eddie and Gunda when Richard still lived with us. When those dogs died, we brought home a Hungarian Sheepdog from Europe, named Bryshya, who was our dog when we divorced. There was also a Siamese cat, Dixie, who lived in David's room. We had him for 18 years.

David had an unusual ability to care for animals. When he was around ten, he insisted that we feed the squirrels, all of which he seemed to have named Peter. He claimed Peter only liked peanuts in the shell. When he was young, he climbed up our magnolia tree in the garden with a banana and a book. One day a bird fell out of the tree and couldn't move. He jumped down, picked it up, took a tongue depressor and bandaged the bird's leg, and put the bird on our kitchen balcony. He fed the bird milk. When the bird grew restless, he removed the dressing and let it fly away. Perhaps it was an early sign that he would be a doctor.

Dr. Dorothy occasionally invited us to her country home in New Jersey. Her home sat on 100 acres of forest. She built three primitive log cabin-style structures from her birch trees in a clearing in the woods. There was a wood burning stove and no running water; it was quite rustic. She was a great cook, an engaging storyteller and, all in all, a terrific hostess. She invited a number of guests for weekends and assigned chores all around. I harvested mint to marinate in a mix of Jack Daniels and sugar for the mint juleps she concocted. Others chopped wood for the stove. David absolutely loved being there. He always volunteered to fetch water because he found salamanders at the well, which he'd stuff into his pockets.

I took the kids into New York City whenever I had a free weekend: to museums, Serendipity for hot chocolate, to plays and to concerts. Sometimes we just wandered through the city together. I scheduled one opera and one Broadway show every year. We'd have dinner and a concert or play. I wanted my kids to learn literature and culture. Young people today like different kinds of music, but I feel that you have to first learn classical music. If you have never listened to Beethoven's 3rd symphony, you haven't heard good music at all. And Tchaikovsky! I thought they should be exposed to classical music, opera and theater. We saw *Carmen, Fiddler on the Roof, Raisin in the Sun*, and many wonderful Broadway plays and lots of great concerts. I planned very carefully for shows that would appeal to them.

One day, when David was away at college, and when Michelle and Pauline were a bit older, I bought tickets to a premiere performance of Nureyev, the foremost Russian ballet dancer at the time. I explained to both of them that by the time they could fully appreciate his mastery, he would be too old to perform. At the concert we sat across from Mick Jagger of the Rolling Stones, so Pauline and Michelle were too preoccupied with the rock star to focus on the dancing. Michelle asked the Mick Jagger for an autograph on Nureyev's program, which she still has framed today.

I was very lucky to have such intelligent children who were interested in learning from me and who could appreciate the value of what I had to offer them as their mother.

Chapter 9

A Career and Family

In the wake of my divorce, having a place to work as wonderful as Columbia was a blessing. I often thought that I landed in the best workplace imaginable. The salary was low (even lower for women) and the demands were high, but the educational possibilities were limitless. And the opportunity to work with so many intelligent doctors was really a privilege. Many of them had written books on pediatrics. Some of them even named many of the syndromes they were treating because they discovered them. I remember one day sitting in a cafeteria between Dr. Riley and Dr. Day, the doctors who discovered and named the Riley-Day syndrome. I said, "Oh my God, I'm having lunch with a syndrome." They laughed.

I increasingly felt that my profession was tailored to me. I had to work extremely hard and make difficult life sacrifices, but it was worth it to help cure patients, or at the very least, reduce their suffering. I regularly thought of how Galina, the doctor from my gulag in Siberia, did all she could to improve the lot of my family and the other prisoners. She remained an inspiration for me.

As a physician, I started in pediatrics. After my residency, I spent a year in general pediatric pathology with Dr. Dorothy Andersen. The education was quite general, but her special interests included Celiac's disease and Cystic Fibrosis (CF). Dorothy was the doctor who first described CF in a pediatric journal in 1939. She learned while working in a Celiac clinic that a portion of her patients with Celiac's who followed prescribed diets showed no improvement. She discovered there was a different issue with those children, and that it was actually CF—which she and a resident of hers discovered was exhibited by salty skin. Together they developed a test by placing a patch on a patient, then analyzing the sodium content of his/her sweat, which it turned out was always higher in CF patients.

Dr. Dorothy was an incredible mentor. She understood my potential and helped me reach it by challenging me from the beginning. She forced me to teach anatomy and embryology of the heart to a group of twelve American medical students. "I'm a foreigner and I speak with an accent," I protested. "Lecturing has nothing to do with any of this," she said. "It has to do with whether you know your subject or not. And I think you do." She suggested that if someone asked an esoteric question, I should simply say that I don't know the answer, and to remember who asked it and make sure I ask that same person a very simple question. The scenario occurred on my first day of class, and I followed her advice exactly. I never heard challenging questions afterward. When we finished the course, the students thanked me and invited me to lunch. And they knew their embryology.

Dorothy also tasked me with reviewing years of papers on Celiac disease, since the relevant literature was written in German by Dutch scientists. After several days in Columbia's library, I returned with sixty different works on Celiac disease. "Very good. Now go back and double check the references," she responded. I thought I'd drop dead because it was summer and the library was not air-conditioned, but I did it willingly. Dorothy and I ultimately wrote four papers together.

She drew all the illustrations herself. She also taught me how to write medical literature. "Be concise," she emphasized.

As her CF research developed, Dorothy called me when she was shorthanded in her clinic and asked if I'd be willing to work Thursday mornings once I finished my residency at Babies Hospital. How could I say no? I was quickly hooked. The patients were amazing young children who matured so quickly because of their struggles. Dorothy noticed that I was staying past noon on Thursdays and began paying me for a full day.

I worked for many years as a pediatrician who specialized in Cystic Fibrosis at Columbia. In time, I became an expert. I handed out my phone number to patients in case of emergencies. Occasionally, I invited patients to stay in my house when they came from out of town, instead of making them spend a night in an emergency room or weeks sleeping in a hospital room chair.

Over the years I lost many patients to the disease. Not because I didn't try my hardest to treat them. There was no cure for the disease and, once diagnosed, we could only do our best to alleviate the pain and delay its progression. In 1991, a gene on the seventh chromosome was discovered to be the cause of CF, which led to advancements in the treatment and diagnosis of the disease (we could now perform genetic testing), but not as much as we had hoped. We tried replacing the genes, but it was unsuccessful. About two years ago, a genetic researcher discovered a way to improve the defective gene and, at present, it looks like this could lead to a cure, which I hope will happen in my lifetime.

What amazes me is that some families still think highly of me even though I was unable to save their children. I am still close with many of the families who lost children to Cystic Fibrosis.

I made it a priority to meet patients with infants at the emergency room when it was necessary to admit their children. In busy emergency rooms patients may wait for hours after signing in. It can be quite challenging for families. I also did my best to treat the people who worked in the garage and the men and women who cleaned the hospital with dignity and respect. That's how I came upon my coveted recipe for spinach pie, which I make every Yom Kippur for break fast. A Greek woman in the cleaning department baked it for me. I loved it so much. I asked her for the recipe and now my kids make it, too.

I wound up at Columbia as a full-time employee for twenty-five years because of the salary and the promise that I could leave at 5p.m. to tend to my children. My first foray into private practice happened after David ruptured his spleen in a sledding accident on his 12th birthday. I rushed him to Columbia where Dr. John Schullinger and Dr. Thomas Vincent Santulli operated on him to save his life. After months of slow recovery, I wanted to send David to Ethical Culture camp for the summer, but it cost $600. I approached Englewood hospital near Leonia and asked if I could pick up extra shifts by covering for doctors, at least until I earned enough money to pay for the camp.

That's when I met Roy Pollock, the Chairman of Pediatrics at Englewood Hospital. Roy let me cover doctor's shifts, but in time offered me a place at his office to see private patients. I still worked at Columbia, but I periodically saw patients in Englewood Hospital, too. Over time, my roster of patients in New Jersey grew. I transferred what had become a burgeoning private practice from Englewood to New York City—to a new office on Park Avenue. I told my patients from Columbia's CF clinic that they could remain at the clinic or see me at my new office. They all came with me. I saw about twenty patients each day.

I still ventured to Columbia regularly because I stayed on the faculty and worked once a week at the pediatric clinic. I would also see patients there for procedures, which I couldn't perform at my office. Staying on the Columbia faculty was important to me. It's a very intellectual place, and I continue to benefit from it. I learned a lot and went to the meetings there every Friday. I also gave occasional talks on Cystic Fibrosis.

Having been a single mother with three children for two years, with a large house and a full time job, Roy Pollack, the director of Englewood Hospital, called to ask me out for dinner. I said yes, and soon we began going out every Thursday night. From day one he wanted to marry me, but I was reluctant. He was divorced from his wife for many years and had two daughters of his own. We dated for about a year. I didn't want to marry again, but I had three children and a house to take care of—and Roy promised that he'd help me raise the kids. After a year I agreed to marry him. We held a small ceremony in the summer of 1977 at a synagogue in Leonia, followed by a reception in a country club.

Roy moved into our home. The kids didn't get along with him that well, and he didn't try very hard to ingratiate himself. They avoided him for the most part, but instead of making it easier for me with the kids, he created a lot of tension. After 17 years of marriage to Roy, we had grown apart, and there wasn't enough between us to make the marriage work. Needless to say, I did not marry well, and in July of 1994, we were divorced.

Chapter Ten

Retirement and Family

Over the past few years, I've said farewell to many loved ones and good friends. Nearly 30 years ago, in 1988, my mother passed away at age 83. She had suffered from diabetes for much of her life. As she grew older, she developed problems that grew increasingly worse and worse. Her mind was fine, but she lost much of her sight and had to have a few toes amputated. My father was unable to care for her on his own. We entertained the idea of an assisted living home, but found them depressing. I visited her every day in her home in Fort Lee to check on her and care for her as best I could. As she grew weaker, she was hospitalized. One day, a doctor arrived with a unit of blood. "What is this for?" she asked. He told her that her blood level was low. "Where I'm going, I don't need this," she said. "Give it to someone who needs it." She was generous up to the very end.

She told me that she was grateful for all of my help. I reminded her of when she gave me her bread to eat in Siberia. "I'm sure you would do the same for your children," she said. "It's nothing special, it's just common sense." I couldn't help but be grateful for the time my mother spent after my divorce, cooking for the children after school and spending quality time with them. I know that her kind and generous influence helped shape each of them into who they are now.

Because my children were raised without Richard for much of their childhood, my father stepped into the role of their father. They enjoyed his company immensely. As the children aged, and my father dealt with the loss of my mother, the two of us developed a special ritual of our own. Once a week, every Sunday, I picked him up and we went to a Korean pastry shop near his home in Fort Lee. After a while, the employees began to recognize us.

When my father suffered a stroke in April 1996, I went with him to Englewood Hospital. He was 93-years-old at the time and had never had an illness up to that point. Once he lost all of his ability to speak, and the ability to move the right side of his body, he felt enough was enough. The children came to bid him farewell. Michelle's son Adam was just two-years-old and he was climbing the bar on my father's bed. My father smiled with amusement. The doctor, a neurologist I knew, told me we could put my father on a respirator. I was with the kids in his room at that point. Unanimously, we said no. He died later that day.

After surviving the Gulag, the steppes of Kazakhstan, the DP camps and immigration to New York City, I was now without my parents for the first time. I know I only survived because of their strength and kindness. I will always be grateful to them.

As for my sister Franny, she relocated to New Mexico in the 1970s. We have not been in contact over the years.

In 2008, after 50 years of working in medicine, I officially retired at the age of 80. I remain a professor emeritus at Columbia, and still attend meetings and conferences. At first, the patients I referred to other doctors still called me after their visits to verify what their doctors said. Those calls eventually stopped, but I remain in touch with many patients. To this day, I attend weddings and all sorts of celebrations for a number of my patients whom I have known for many years.

A decade prior, I moved from my house in Leonia to a nice apartment in Manhattan. I wanted to be near my children in the city, where they all live. I found an apartment on the Upper West Side near my daughter Michelle and close to Columbia Presbyterian Hospital.

I thought living by myself would be very depressing and difficult, especially once I retired. It is neither. How would I fill my days? At work I always had more to do, more to read, more calls to make. But once retired, I suddenly found myself very busy at museums, art history classes, operas and plays. I've been able to make new friends. I also began to spend more of my time cooking for myself. Now that I'm older, preparing dinners takes longer: one whole day to shop, one day to prep and one day to cook. That's why I cook simply. Every now and again I try more elaborate dishes for guests. There are several friends that I like to invite over. And I have finally learned to have groceries delivered by the store.

Aging is not without its pains, of course. In 2005, years after first injuring my knee while playing tennis, my knee gave out and I needed a replacement. I underwent surgery. After a week I was discharged with crutches and a walker. Physical therapy was daily. The discomfort remained significant. Two and a half years afterward the knee swelled up every night, and required ice packs regularly. I needed revision surgery because the first was unsuccessful. I underwent a second surgery, which kept me out of a wheelchair, but couldn't repair the knee as new. Needless to say, I still feel significant pain. My friend Dr. Sylvia Griffith, a retired pediatric cardiologist at Columbia, and I often compare our physical ailments, but we try to talk about issues other than just our health.

After a while I signed up to audit courses at Columbia University. Since I'm still on the faculty, I can take courses for free. Over the years I've taken various courses on the influence of the East and West on Russian art, 19th and 20th century art, postmodern art and femininity, novellas from Cervantes to Kafka to Nabokov and ancient history to learn how the world evolved. It takes a physical and mental effort to take classes, but now I have a more informed perspective when I go to a museum or read books.

Spending my days studying literature and reading the masters brings me back to the little girl I was in the Gulag of Siberia, when reading the works of the best Russian writers, particularly Eugene Onegin by Pushkin, lent to me by Galina the doctor gave me a purpose. I was cold and hungry and treated poorly, and reading was the highlight of my day. And now that I take these courses, they provide a great opportunity to enrich my retirement with knowledge I never had the time to pursue. Of all the luxuries in life, taking these classes is something I truly enjoy.

My children and their families made my transition to Manhattan and to retirement possible with their generosity and care. They've always made me proud. David even followed in my footsteps in medicine, but he did it in his own, independent way. He is now a celebrated doctor on the Lower East Side. Pauline received degrees in Chemistry, Industrial Design and Computer Science. And Michelle became a lawyer and now volunteers for various organizations with underserved youth, the needy in Israel and a Jewish Community Center in Krakow. I was especially pleased that my daughters married dedicated husbands and fathers. Pauline married Michael McCaffery and Michelle married Chip Schorin, both great men. Pauline gave birth to two girls, Lia and Marisa, and Michelle had three boys, Adam, Paul and Marc. I was present at the birth of each grandchild because my daughters asked me to be there. My five grandchildren all became my patients.

I eat Shabbat dinner with Michelle's family every week, and on occasion, my grandchildren join me for meals at my home. Marc and Adam are vegetarians, which has pushed me to learn to cook tofu and to make quinoa taste delicious. I may be of a different generation, but I have a lot in common with my grandchildren. Marc and I speak Yiddish and Russian together. I persuaded all of Michelle's boys to read Eugene Onegin's story by Pushkin, a story I first read while in Siberia. I learn a lot from each grandchild in so many different ways.

I have a fabulous bedroom with a balcony in Michelle and Chip's country house in Connecticut with a balcony. In the luxury of that house, I can't help but be reminded of my time in the Siberian gulag where I experienced the worst living circumstances imaginable. I still can't believe that we adapted to those sub-human conditions. As a doctor, I witnessed how my young CF patients adapted to their chronic pain in order to survive and it reminded me of what I had to do in Siberia. In such states, I could see people's true character, what I liked to think of as their "naked state." My mother revealed herself to me when she gave me her bread ration, and Galina revealed herself to me when she saved my life with care and literature. Because of both of them, I've wanted to do something constructive in this world, to build a life to make up for all of those lost years during the war. I feel, particularly as a doctor to CF patients, I have contributed fully to help others throughout my life.

Epilogue

Returning

I returned to my hometown, Dubienka, in 1996 with Michelle and Chip for the first time since the war. I was hesitant about returning, but since my children cared enough about me to want to see where I was born, I felt an obligation. I agreed to travel on the condition that Adam, a toddler at the time, stayed home. I was concerned with what awaited us in Dubienka and did not want to bring my very young grandson into an unknown situation.

We drove with a driver from Krakow to Dubienka. There was just one store selling fruit and canned goods in town. Jews had owned most of the stores when I was a child. When we pulled up near my old family home, a woman asked our driver, "What do they want?" She didn't know I spoke Polish. "We don't want anything," I said in the language of my childhood. "I just want my children to see where I used to live."

Memories flooded back to me as we stood on my childhood street. The park across the street with the statue of General Kosciuszko hadn't been cared for properly. The synagogue was gone and now the site was a bus station and the Jewish cemetery was razed. Homes were built upon the site. The whole town looked depressing, and most of its residents were old.

I didn't recognize our old apartment building, once a red brick facade that we were told was stuccoed over by the Soviets. I couldn't go upstairs because the stairs were in poor condition. My daughter Michelle went to take a photo of an old wooden house near my family's home that the Goldberg family had owned. "It's very rude to take a photo of someone else's house," a woman yelled at us through the window.

"Tell her the Goldbergs wouldn't have minded," Michelle said to me. I translated.

"We bought this place from the Jewish family who lived here," said the grandmother of the home, who came to the window defensively to explain to us. I'm fairly certain that they didn't buy it from the Goldbergs, but I saw no point in arguing at that time.

We met Gabriela Poliwczak, a lovely Polish woman in town who was very interested in the Jewish history of Dubienka. She invited us to her home for tea with her children. Many of the town's young people had left due to an absence of opportunities, she explained. Dubienka was now populated with mostly retired and elderly people. Gabriela walked with us to the River Bug so I could show Michelle and Chip where my family crossed to safety from the Nazis. On the way back to Krakow, we visited the concentration camps Majdanek and Auschwitz, both very difficult experiences for all of us. I fell ill at the gates of the camps. It was an awful experience to see how methodical and organized the Nazis were in killing six million people. We later flew to Prague and heard James Galway in a concert at the Prague Castle. It was very poignant to have a day where we witnessed the worst of mankind in the morning and the best of mankind with a beautiful concert that evening, showing the heights people can reach when focusing their creativity and energy on good instead of evil.

As I returned to the U.S., I was sad to have replaced my pleasant memories of Dubienka with images of the gloomy present. But I was heartened that I could show my children the place of my origins. I could also appreciate how living in the United States has been the greatest privilege. Had I stayed in Dubienka, I'm not sure I would have been able to travel the world, pursue an education and become a doctor. But who knows. The war had interrupted and transformed our lives in such an extraordinary way. Now, my children and grandchildren are Americans with all the freedoms imaginable. When I was in a Siberian gulag, it never occurred to me that I would be where I am today, studying at Columbia and taking my grandchildren to operas.

Ten years later, in 2004, I returned to Poland with Michelle and my grandchildren Adam and Lia, ages 10 and 13 at the time. Dubienka was the same, but Adam and Lia wanted to see it. We met with Gabriela and walked again to the River Bug. "This is not the town I lived in," I told Adam and Lia. "It's a ghost of the town." When I saw a man working in the garden near my home, I asked him if he knew my childhood friend, Halina Golczewska, and if she still lived nearby. He told me she had married and moved to Lublin and he did not know her family name. I considered trying to find her, but I wasn't sure if Halina wanted to be reminded of me. I wasn't sure if I wanted to remember her, either.

Then we went to see Belzec, an extermination camp, on the way back to Krakow. Later on, we spent a day in the salt mines of Wieliczka and visited the Wawel Castle, Jagiellonian University and Copernicus's study. We also toured the Jewish quarter of Krakow called Kazimeirz where we met with a tour guide named Agnieszka Legutko, who remains a dear friend to this day and is now the Director of Yiddish Studies at Columbia University. It was wonderful to have my grandchildren with me.

I returned once again to Dubienka again in June 2015 with David, Pauline and her daughter Marisa, and Michelle and her sons Paul and Marc. Even though it's not the same village of my childhood, I was pleased to show them where I live. We met with Gabriela again who had arranged a meeting with the mayor of the region for us, as well as a presentation of photographs of Jewish life in Dubienka before the war at the local school. We then had a wonderful lunch at Gabriela's home, along with two other women close to my age. For this trip, my daughter Michelle had tracked down Halina and discovered that she now lives in Poznan, Poland with her husband. Halina and I spoke just before this trip to Poland. It was the first time we had spoken since 1939. We made plans to meet halfway between Poznan and Warsaw but she cancelled the night before. Her daughter said it was too difficult for her mother to meet with me. I am not sure why but that's the way it is.

I have more negative views of Poland than my children have. The new generation in Poland doesn't have that same burden. They weren't punished unfairly for being born into Judaism as I had been. But now they want to see where I was born, so I was glad to go. We also visited the new Polin: the Museum of the History of Polish Jews, the museum of the 1000 year history of Jews in Poland and had dinner with Barbara Kirschenblatt Gimblett, the curator of the museum. In addition, we visited the JCC Krakow where there is a renewal of Jewish life particularly for the next generations, and where Michelle is now on the Friends Board. The Polin Museum, along with the JCC Krakow, are positive signs that the significant Jewish history of Poland will now be explained showing how the Jewish people in Poland contributed to the good of the country and to the Polish legacy.

Acknowledgements

Thank you to Dr. John Schullinger, who inspired me to finally write down my life story. I would fill up yellow lined notepads with handwritten chapters and mail them to John in Vermont, who in turn would type up the notes for me. Then John would mail his typed pages back to me, along with the yellow handwritten notes. We worked this way for 21 chapters! So thank you to John for inspiring me to write my story.

Then a huge thank you to Jeffrey Yoskowitz, who edited and compiled the book. He reviewed the 21 chapters very closely with me. We would meet for hours to put the story in chronological order, as well as fill in some of the blanks or delve more deeply into some of the chapters in my life. An enormous debt of gratitude for his input and guidance. We would, of course, also speak about gefilte fish and kreplach, and other Eastern European food. He never left my home hungry.

I also wish to thank Sherrie Nickol for taking my author photo. She is a very thoughtful and talented photographer. Additional thanks to Ruth Calderon, Ellen Heuman and Ron Gutman and Pete Putzel for their comments. In addition, thank you to Agnieszka Legutko, for being our tour guide in the Kazimeirz quarter of Krakow in 2004 and for being our dear friend.

And most important, I thank my three children and my two sons-in-law – Pauline, David, Michelle, Michael and Chip -- and five grandchildren – Lia, Marisa, Adam, Paul and Marc. All of my children and grandchildren have been to Dubienka. After our visits, I believe they all had a better sense of my life before the war in my shtetl Dubienka on the River Bug.

Thank you again to all.

Warmest regards,
Celia

My parents and me, around 1929.

My maternal uncle, Shepsel, his wife, Leah, and their daughter Sonya.

My uncle Shepsel with his daughter Sonya

My maternal uncle, Fivel, sometime before the war.

A Jewish New Year's card from the DP camp, with
my parents, my sister, and me, around 1947.

My parents along with other survivors in the DP camp, at a memorial.

My mother with Franny.

Me with my mother Ita after the war.

My graduating class from University of Berne Medical
School (I am front row, just right of center).

My father.

From right to left, Irinka, a colleague from Poland,
another colleague Dr. Blanka Schneid, and me.

My father in New York City, around 1955.

Myself, late 1950s.

Ita, Paul, Celia, Franny, Anna, and Frank, around 1955.

My father in Central Park with Franny and Pauline, around 1958.

Dr. Max Weinstein, a colleague at Columbia,
and me at a wedding, late 1950's.

My parents with my children, around 1962.

Me with Michelle and our wonderful Bernese
Mountain Dog named Eddie, 1962.

My children in Jerusalem, from left to right,
Michelle, David, and Pauline, around 1967.

My daughter, Pauline, my professor from Bern, Dr. Walthard,
and me, in front of the Guggenheim, early 1960's.

My children, from left to right, Michelle,
Pauline, and David, late 1970's.

My grandchildren, about 2006.

Me with my children and son in laws, about 1998.

Here I am visiting Dubienka in 2004 with my Michelle, Lia and
Adam, with Barbara and her family, who live in Dubienka.

Me with Harry Belafonte.

Family photo with my children, spouses,
grandchildren and their dogs, 2010.

In front of my childhood home in Dubienka, Poland with my children, and three grandchildren — Marisa, Paul and Marc, June 2015.

About the Author

Celia Ores is a Polish born Holocaust survivor and was a pediatrician for over 50 years. Her memoir details her life in Dubienka, Poland as a child, then a prisoner in a Siberian gulag and a labor camp near Alma-Ata, Kazakhstan. After the war, she attended medical school in Switzerland and moved to New York City to be a pediatrican at Columbia Presbyterian Medical Center. She is now retired taking numerous art history and literature classes at Columbia University, and enjoying concerts and opera at Lincoln Center. She lives in New York City, as do her three children and five grandchildren.

Made in the USA
Middletown, DE
02 March 2020